A Dog Tries to Kiss the Sky

7 SHORT PLAYS

Works by Douglas Messerli / Kier Peters

Kier Peters

A Dog Tries to Kiss THE Sky

7 SHORT PLAYS

GREEN INTEGER
KØBENHAVN & LOS ANGELES
2003

GREEN INTEGER BOOKS
Edited by Per Bregne
København / Los Angeles

Distributed in the United States by Consortium Book
Sales and Distribution, 1045 Westgate Drive, Suite 90
Saint Paul, Minnesota 55114-1065

(323) 857-1115 / http://www.greeninteger.com

First Edition 2003
Copyright ©2003 by Kier Peters
All rights reserved.
For all professional and amateur production and reading rights
please contact the author c/o Green Integer,
6022 Wilshire Boulevard, Suite 200A, Los Angeles, CA 90036

Design: Per Bregne
Typography & Cover: Trudy Fisher
Photograph: Kier Peters by Howard Fox

LIBRARY OF CONGRESS CATALOGING IN PUBLICATION DATA
Peters, Kier [Douglas Messerli] [1947]
A Dog Tries to Kiss the Sky: Seven Short Plays
ISBN: 1-931243-30-1
p. cm — Green Integer 89
I. Title II. Series

Green Integer books are published for Douglas Messerli
Printed in the United States of America on acid-free paper.

CONTENTS

PAST PRESENT FUTURE TENSE

ACT I

Tulips: An Elocutionary Piece

[*In Philadelpia there stands a cardboard table, doily-covered, on which is centered a vase of real tulips. To the sides of the table are matching, rather handsomely upholstered cardboard chairs. Near one she stands. In the other sits a not inattentive man.*]

SHE: The whole house smells of tulips.

HE: Yes.

SHE: I'm allergic to pollen, you'll recall.

HE: Oh?

SHE: I'm certain to be having an asthma attack.

HE: Really?

SHE: And headaches. You know how bad they get.

HE: No.

SHE: Remember last year?

HE: I guess.

SHE: Migraines. Even the doctor couldn't cure them.

HE: Oh, yes.

SHE: I get cross.

HE: Oh dear.

SHE: And in June it gets worse.

HE: Oh my!

SHE: I'm nearly dead by the end of July.

HE: That bad?

SHE: Then hayfever August creeps in.

HE: Good Lord!

SHE: And I can hardly breathe.

HE: Horrible!

SHE: I collapse.

[*He gasps.*]

SHE: You call the doctor.

HE: Help!

SHE: I'm rushed to the clinic.

HE: Hurry!

SHE: Oxygen is desperately pumped into my lungs.

HE: Ah!

SHE: My pulse returns.

HE: Thank heaven!

SHE: Miraculously, I live.

HE: Of course.

SHE: So?

HE: You must recuperate!

SHE: Well?

HE: We run away to Arizona.

SHE: Certainly not.

HE: To France?

SHE: Perhaps.

HE: We have reservations at the Claridge.

SHE: We do?

HE: We fly into Orly.

SHE: Obviously.

HE: We taxi into Paris, and rush up to our suite.

SHE: Yes?

HE: We follow the porter across the room as he swings open the doors of our veranda.

SHE: Fine.

HE: Below is the Champs Élysées.

SHE: Very good.

HE: The sun is setting over the city.

SHE: Marvelous!

HE: We order dinner, champagne.

SHE: Not bad.

HE: It's terribly expensive.

SHE: Better be!

HE: I suggest a walk.

SHE: You do?

HE: In the Tuileries.

SHE: Alright.

HE: It's so lovely this time of year, this hour of night.

SHE: Ummmmm.

HE: I take your hand. Your head falls to my shoulder.

SHE: It might.

HE: Lovers surround us.

SHE: Yes.

HE: The air is scented with the perfume of roses.

SHE: How *could* you?

HE: I forgot!

SHE: I leave you.

HE: No!

SHE: I take a night train to Nice.

HE: Please!

SHE: I sit, tapping the anger out through my fingers.

HE: Forgive me!

SHE: A man is situated across.

HE: Who?

SHE: A Frenchman. He smiles. I become self-conscious. My fingers stop.

HE: Don't!

SHE: He smiles again.

HE: How rude!

SHE: I smile back.

HE: You're cruel!

SHE: He nods and leans towards me.

HE: Outrageous!

SHE: Madame, is something troubling you? he asks.

HE: Improper!

SHE: I do not mean to pry, he adds. I say, yes, I'm desperate.

HE: Evidently!

SHE: My husband tried to kill me.

HE: A lie!

SHE: He gasps. How could anyone have even thought to harm such a beauty?

HE: Unoriginal beast!

SHE: I blush.

HE: Never!

SHE: He introduces himself.

HE: Finally!

SHE: He is the Count de Marquis.

HE: A fake!

SHE: He has a villa on the Riviera.

HE: Big deal!

SHE: He suggests I change my plans, that I come visit his magnificent estate.

HE: You agree?

SHE: I tell him that I'll consider it.

HE: He pressures?

SHE: Why shouldn't he?

HE: Whore!

SHE: In his arms, I'm protected from such crude remarks.

HE: And reality.

SHE: Can't hear.

HE: I've completely forgotten you.

SHE: Good.

HE: I return to Philadelphia.

SHE: Fine.

HE: I flounder for a bit.

SHE: Nothing new.

HE: But soon I find a job with a law firm.

SHE: Without schooling?

HE: As a clerk.

SHE: Dreamer!

HE: They like my work, put me through night–
    school.

SHE: Fools.

HE: I study long and arduously. Soon I'm ready
    for the bar exams.

SHE: You fail.

HE: The second time, I pass.

SHE: With help.

HE: I'm all alone.

SHE: No women?

HE: I gave them up.

SHE: You're celibate!?

HE: For awhile. One night, however, I'm invited
    to a party where I meet an old friend.

SHE: A tart!

HE: We talk. We've a lot in common. I fall in love.

SHE: Mousy thing!

HE: Black hair. Olive-skinned.

SHE: Cheap.

HE: His name is Paul Durand.

    [*She gasps.*]

HE: I don't expect that you could ever understand.
    But it doesn't matter. For all I know you may
    be dead.

SHE: I'm not!

HE: At any rate, we're very happy.

13

SHE: Pansy!

HE: He's athletic.

SHE: You make me sick.

HE: In Nice?

SHE: François and I take a trip.

HE: Philly?

SHE: London, for awhile.

HE: You're bored.

SHE: A bit.

HE: With François?

SHE: With everything.

HE: Another woman?

SHE: He could never do that!

HE: And you?

SHE: Not without his knowledge.

HE: His approval?

SHE: We're a modern couple. We've a mature relationship.

HE: But now . . . ?

SHE: I can't explain how I feel. Depressed.

HE: Rejected.

SHE: I haven't heard about your being queer.

HE: That's safe.

SHE: But then I decide to return to Philadelphia.

HE: Alone?

SHE: For a visit.

HE: Miss me?

SHE: To see my mother.

HE: In Indiana?

SHE: She's moved out here since.

HE: Convenient.

SHE: I stay with her for a few days.

HE: My regards.

SHE: She's in good health. I'm rather enjoying myself.

HE: Until?

SHE: Susan — you remember her — calls one night and suggests we go out dancing.

HE: No husband?

SHE: She's been divorced.

HE: Watch out!

SHE: She frequents a very nice singles' bar.

HE: For pickups.

SHE: Susan, I say, I'm not really the singles' bar type. She says, Oh you're so hung up. Your ex-husband has stripped away all your confidence.

HE: Same bitch.

SHE: So, I join her. It's a little place not far from where I used to live.

HE: My house.

SHE: I dance for a little, and then I wander over to the bar.

HE: Your usual?

SHE: Martini on the rocks . . . .

HE: Three olives.

SHE: You remembered!

HE: *Prosit!*

SHE: To us!

> [*He laughs.*]

SHE: [*Angrily*] Suddenly I see this man looking in the mirror.

HE: At himself?

SHE: Our eyes meet.

He: You wink.

SHE: I look away.

HE: You flirt.

SHE: But then I think, he's not so bad. And being a modern woman I go up to him and ask if he wants to dance.

HE: You castrate.

SHE: He smiles, but declines. He seems so shy.

HE: Terrorized.

SHE: But he does ask me to join him. And although Susan and I soon have to leave, he gives me his number.

HE: A conventioneer?

SHE: He's a Philadelphian.

HE: He's doomed.

SHE: So the next afternoon, I call and we make a date.

HE: And London?

SHE: François's gone on to Rome.

HE: Fortunate.

SHE: I'm surprised to find how really shy my new friend is. He's so humble, so gentle. I suspect he's married. And when I ask, he admits.

HE: Tsk tsk.

SHE: But, of course, one thing leads to another.

HE: I expect.

SHE: And we find ourselves getting to like each other.

HE: Not love?

SHE: And finally, it's love.

HE: Once more!

SHE: My friend decides to leave his mate. It's only then I find out. His name is . . . Paul Durand.

HE: Damn you!

SHE: So François — whom I never married — receives a telegram.

HE: Savage!

SHE: And Paul and I rent a house on Society Hill.

HE: With what?

SHE: I help him get a job — a publishing firm.

HE: He's illiterate!

SHE: You always berate him. Deny his talents! Underrate his worth.

HE: You're mistaken!

SHE: I love him.

HE: Prove it!

SHE: I won't give him up.

HE: You must!

SHE: He won't go back to you.

HE: But he will go back to men.

SHE: No!

HE: So we're back where we started from.

SHE: Don't!

HE: It's destiny.

SHE: Please.

HE: You crawl home to me.

SHE: I refuse!

HE: You've no money, no job, nowhere else.

SHE: It's unfair!

HE: Isn't it.

SHE: I hate you.

HE: I know.

SHE: I loathe the very sight of you.

HE: Of course.

SHE: I can't even say your name without wanting to vomit.

HE: No doubt.

SHE: You humiliate me.

HE: Impossible.

SHE: You torture me.

HE: Perhaps.

SHE: You've never loved anyone.

HE: Once.

SHE: [*For an instant, she's speechless. Then, recovering, she points her finger at the tulips.*] Get rid of them!

HE: You're right.

[*He takes the tulips from the vase, and leaves the room.*]

ACT II

Lies: A Drawing Room Farce

[*She is moving now. She is taking a position. She straddles a chair. She is going nowhere tonight. He is standing. He looks at the ocean. She crosses to him. He dos not observe, back to her, lost in reverie. She sits down. She stays seated. Turning, he comes back.*]

HER: What are you thinking about?

HIM: Nothing.

[*She says nothing.*]

HIM: The sea.
HER: Oh, I see.
HIM: It is such a pretty sight.
HER: Really.
HIM: Yes, come look.
HER: [*She rises and looks.*] Yes.
HIM: Isn't it a pretty sight?
HER: Yes.
HIM: You didn't sleep last night.
HER: Oh I slept. Some.
HIM: I'm going out for a swim.
HER: It's almost time for dinner.
HIM: Then I shall have an appetite. [*He goes out.*]
   [*She stays. In her chair. She stands. She paces, impatient for him to come back.*]
   [*He comes back, shaking his face. He towels his body off.*]
   [*She sits to wait.*]
HER: It is time to go to dinner.
HIM: Then we shall go.
HER: You must dress.
HIM: Must I?
HER: You must dress.
HIM: Then I shall.
HER: Good. [*She waits. She stands. She paces.*]
   [*He comes back into the room. She sits.*]

HER: Now it is time to go.

HIM: I must put on some cologne.

HER: Must you?

HIM: Yes.

HER: Then do.
  [*He does.*]

HER: Now it is time to go.

HIM: Mightn't we stay and cook a steak?

HER: We promised to join our friends.

HIM: We could call them.

HER: They are expecting us.
  [*She stands. He sits.*]

HIM: You could say I was ill.

HER: I could not.

HIM: You might.

HER: Are you ill?

HIM: No.

HER: Then we must go.
  [*She sits. He stands. He moves to her, putting his hands upon her head.*]

HIM: Mightn't we lie a bit?

HER: I don't like to.

HIM: But you have?

HER: Yes.

HIM: And I have too.

HER: Yes.

[*He sits.*]

HIM: And you to me?

HER: Yes.

[*She stands. She goes to the window. Yes, the sea is quite nice. But it is getting dark and difficult to witness it. The waves roll in.*]

HER: It is getting dark.

HIM: Yes.

HER: And growing late.

HIM: And we shall be.

HER: Yes.

HIM: Was it serious?

HER: What?

HIM: The lie.

HER: [*She turns back into the room. She comes to the chair.*] There have been many.

HIM: Many lies?

HER: Many.

HIM: I have told many too.

HER: But I do not like to.

HIM: Neither do I.

HER: So let us go.

HIM: I want to know.

HER: It is very difficult.

HIM: [*He stands. He goes to the window.*] Yes, it is very difficult.

HER: I have had an affair.
HIM: Yes. I have also had one.
HER: Yes. I guessed you had.
HIM: With whom?
HER: Does it matter?
HIM: No. It does not.
HER: And with whom did you?
HIM: You can imagine.
HER: Yes, I can.
   [*He tries to penetrate the dark.*]
HER: But I don't care really.
HIM: Neither do I.
HER: I care only about us.
HIM: And so do I.
HER: But we are not here. Not here really.
HIM: [*He comes back to the chair.*] I am.
HER: No you are not.
HIM: I am. But it is so very difficult.
HER: Then I am not.
HIM: You have been.
HER: [*She stands.*] But I have tried.
HIM: [*He goes to the bar.*] A gin?
HER: Yes. A gin.
   [*He makes a scotch.*]
HIM: I have tried to come back.
HER: Did I prevent you?

HIM: Yes.

> [*He makes a gin. He brings her the gin. He drinks, and she.*]

HER: We better call them.

HIM: If you must.

HER: [*She phones.*] Betty, we will not be joining you tonight. We are having an important talk.

> [*Betty says,* Oh, we were so counting on the two of you.]

HER: But we need to be together. Just the two of us tonight.

> [It sounds romantic, *Betty says.*]

HER: But it's not.

> [*She hangs up.*]

> [*He is at the window again. But he can no longer see through the dark.*]

HIM: Are you still in love?

HER: No, I am not.

HIM: Were you?

HER: No, I don't think I was.

HIM: With me?

HER: Are you still in love?

HIM: With you?

HER: Yes.

HIM: I think I am.

HER: I think you want to be.

HIM: And you?

HER: No.

HIM: Do you want to be?

HER: I'm not sure. I have tried.

HIM: Unsuccessfully.

HER: Yes.

HIM: Do you think you can again?
      [*He sits. She stands.*]

HER: No. I don't think so.

HIM: You're thinking of leaving then.

HER: [*She turns.*] Do you want me to?

HIM: No. I don't want you to go.

HER: Then I shan't.

HIM: Good.

HER: Yes.

HIM: But eventually . . . .

HER: I might. I think I can live without loving
      someone. But can you?

HIM: But I *do* love you.

HER: You want to. But I need to know can you live
      without me loving you?

HIM: I think I can.

HER: You'd be free, of course.

HIM: Yes.

HER: To see him. Or anyone.

HIM: I'm not sure I want.

HER: You shall be free, in any event.

HIM: Do you want to?

HER: No. But I might.

HIM: You might.

HER: So, what shall we do?

HIM: I'll get the steaks.

HER: Yes. It is dinnertime. [*She sits.*]
[*He rises. He leaves the room. He comes back.*]

HIM: I put the steaks on the countertop.

HER: I'll start the barbecue. [*She stands.*]

HIM: [*He sits.*] But I'm not really hungry.

HER: I'm sorry.

HIM: I know.

HER: Still, I am.

HIM: And I am also.

HER: Yes.

HIM: Can I ask, when did you stop?

HER: Stop?

HIM: Loving.

HER: Oh, I suppose when I realized you didn't love me.

HIM: But I do love you. I did.

HER: You wanted to. You desire it.

HIM: Why do you keep saying that?

HER: Because it's true.

HIM: No, I refuse to believe you.

HER: It's not just the sex.

HIM: [*He rises.*] That's nonsense.

HER: It's the personality. Just being in the same room.

[*She sips.*]

HIM: I don't think that's true. I hate almost all of his habits.

HER: That's what you said.

HIM: I don't comprehend.

HER: You don't mind if I smoke?

HIM: No. [*She takes out a cigarette.*]

HER: You hate him for jingling his keys.

HIM: It drives me crazy.

HER: Me too.

HIM: Yes?

HER: Don't you see?

HIM: See what? [*He goes to the window.*]

HER: I think I'm going to be sick.

HIM: Really? [*He comes over to check her pulse.*] Do you have a fever?

HER: No.

HIM: It's probably just the stress.

HER: Yes.

HIM: You need an aspirin.

HER: Could you get me one?

[*He leaves the room and brings one back.*]

[*She takes it, sips.*]

HER: You laid him down on the couch and stroked his head.

HIM: Who?

HER: You turned him over and rubbed his back.

HIM: Well, he was really ill!

HER: So his wife said. I think she might have wanted to take him home.

HIM: I shouldn't wonder.

HER: What do you mean?

HIM: With you playing foot tag with him under the table the entire night.

HER: Do you think she noticed?

[*He looks out.*]

HER: Poor Betty.

HIM: Yes.

HER: He's not very attractive.

HIM: [*He turns back in.*] No, he's not.

HER: You're much better looking.

HIM: Thank you.

HER: And I think I've got it all over Betty.

HIM: Oh, you do. You do.

[*She sips.*]

HIM: Would you like another gin?

HER: Yes.

[*He makes another gin. He makes another scotch.*]

HER: And those terrible children!

HIM: Brats!

HER: I should turn on the barbecue.

HIM: Are you feeling up to it?

HER: Yes.

[*She stands.*] Both of us are fools.

HIM: Yes. But you're right.

HER: I am?

HIM: About my being in love.

HER: You are in love then?

HIM: I want to be.

HER: With him?

HIM: With you.

HER: But you're not.

HIM: No. Evidently.

HER: And you are with him?

HIM: I can't answer that. [*He goes to the bar.*]

HER: You must. If I'm to stay, you must.

HIM: [*He sits.*] He has a big penis.

HER: Yes.

HIM: And we did have good sex.

HER: So did *we.*

HIM: That stands for something.

HER: Not very much.

HIM: No. I guess.

HER: He's a good conversationalist.

HIM: Excellent.

HER: And he makes you feel you're at the center of his thoughts.

HIM: Yes.

HER: It's horrible to watch Betty try to keep up!

HIM: Poor Betty. So, do you still love him? [*He drinks.*]

HER: No.

HIM: Are you certain?

HER: Oh, I think of it from time to time. Think of him. Like a ditty you can't get out your mind.

HIM: That serious.

HER: No, it's not serious.

HIM: I think it is.

HER: Besides, he's hot for you!

HIM: No he's not.

HER: No? Every time you're in the room his eyes begin to flutter.

HIM: I never noticed.

HER: When he's looking into your eyes, they stop.

HIM: Sounds like an affliction.

HER: It is.

HIM: [*He drinks.*] I'm not the cause.

HER: [*She stands.*] And then, when he gazes at you that way, I suddenly feel this wave of love pass right through me.

HIM: For him?

HER: For you.

HIM: You do?

HER: But only then. At this very moment I couldn't care less.

HIM: I was jealous.

HER: When?

HIM: Whenever I thought of the two of you.

HER: Jealous of me?

HIM: Jealous of him.

HER: Really?

HIM: With the way he could have you, while I couldn't ever satisfy you as much.

HER: No.

HIM: I know. You don't have to explain.

HER: I wasn't going to.

HIM: I wish you would.

HER: What?

HIM: Explain. Not why he is better than me. I know all about that. But why I could never satisfy you.

HER: Who said?

HIM: What?

HER: I wasn't satisfied.

HIM: It's obvious.

HER: To whom?

HIM: To me. To him. Even to Betty.

HER: Really. [*She stands.*] But it isn't, wasn't your fault.

HIM: I don't understand.

HER: I mean, with him it wasn't much better.

HIM: [*He stands.*] I'm sorry. With us it was so good.

HER: You mean, with you and him.

HIM: Yes. And for me, you.

HER: But one has to choose.

HIM: Choose?

HER: It has become necessary. [*She goes to the window.*]

HIM: [*He drinks.*] But I was the one who loved you.

HER: So you said.

HIM: And you were the one who wanted out.

HER: Yes.

HIM: And you no longer do? [*He stands.*]

HER: [*She sits. She stands. She sips her drink.*] No.

HIM: It is time for the steaks.

HER: Yes. I shall start the barbecue.

HIM: Or maybe we should join our friends.

HER: Perhaps.

HIM: I think we should.

HER: It was impolite.

[*She picks up the phone and dials.*] Betty, we're on our way.

[*She puts the phone down again.*]

HIM: He *is* handsome.

HER: Yes he is.

HIM: And you do love him, don't you?

HER: Yes.

HIM: And I do too.

HER: Yes.

HIM: Good, I'm glad we got that off our chests.

HER: Yes. And Betty is very nice.

[*They remain standing, undecided to stay in or go out.*]

ACT III

Matador: A Romance

[*A man and a woman are alone.*]

WOMAN: Once upon a time we were very happy.

MAN: We sure were!

WOMAN: And then we were not happy.

MAN: No.

WOMAN: For a very long time.

MAN: Yes.

WOMAN: And I went away.

MAN: And I stayed.

WOMAN: And you went off.

MAN: And you remained.

WOMAN: And then one day . . .

MAN: One day we met along our ways . . .

WOMAN: Our various ways . . .

MAN: And I said, I miss you. And you said . . .

WOMAN: I was thinking the same thing.

MAN: Isn't it amazing!

WOMAN: We always did think alike.

MAN: And that's why we fought.

WOMAN: It was like fighting with myself.

MAN: So I became a tyrant.

WOMAN: And I became a bitch.

MAN: And night and day we argued over everything.

WOMAN: Everything! Even cottage cheese!

MAN: Oh, I remember that!

WOMAN: And the kitchen sink.

MAN: You scrubbed it with a brillo pad.

WOMAN: And it got scratched.

MAN: It was a stupid thing to do!

WOMAN: You insisted upon porcelain.

MAN: I hate the look of stainless steel.

WOMAN: And our friends!

MAN: Yes, we fought mostly over them.

WOMAN: You wanted to have an affair with the
husband of my girlfriend.

MAN: And you *had* an affair with him.

WOMAN: And then you did.

MAN: And then you had an affair with his wife.

WOMAN: And you tried to butt in!

MAN: I wasn't attracted to Betty at all.

WOMAN: Neither was I to Paul.

MAN: Nor was he to you!

WOMAN: So it drove me mad.

MAN: I got jealous and went insane.

WOMAN: I wouldn't say anything for months.

MAN: I couldn't stop shouting.

WOMAN: I became an alcoholic.

MAN: I checked into the loony bin.

WOMAN: I attended meetings of AA.

MAN: I got involved in group therapy.

WOMAN: I met lots of men.

MAN: I went to bed with my shrink.

WOMAN: I confessed to drinking far more than I drank.

MAN: I made up stories, dreams, fantasies.

WOMAN: I lived out my wildest imaginations of motorcycle men.

MAN: It drove me to drugs.

WOMAN: I went into a frenzy.

MAN: And gradually my money ran out.

WOMAN: I could no long reach a sexual climax.

MAN: My shrink pronounced me cured.

WOMAN: My mother said I ought to move in with her again.

MAN: My father died.

WOMAN: I had dreams of having sex with my brother.

MAN: I stopped shaving.

WOMAN: I grew a beard.

MAN: I drifted through the streets.

WOMAN: I joined a circus.

MAN: I peed right out in public.

WOMAN: I went to bed with a midget.

MAN: I urinated on myself.

WOMAN: I let the midget shit upon my breasts.

MAN: I wanted you.

WOMAN: I wanted out.

MAN: While jacking off, I hung myself.

WOMAN: I slit my wrists and sat down in the river bed.

MAN: A boozer cut me loose.

WOMAN: The tide carried me down to a doctor's boat.

[*They embrace.*]

MAN: But every night I see that rope. [*Out of thin air he produces a rope.*]

36

WOMAN: When I come to the river everything turns red.

[*The man takes up a red-checked tablecloth and waves it in front of the woman. Behind it he holds the hangman's rope.*]

[*The woman flares her nostrils, attacking it like a bull. The man plays the matador, and as she breaks through the cloth he catches her neck in the noose.*]

MAN: Gotcha!

WOMAN: [*Suddenly realizing her plight, she rears up in his face and comes down hard, knocking him to the ground, trampling him.*]

WOMAN: [*over the bleeding, mutilated body of the murderous matador*] And then we met on our ways in and out.

MAN: [*groaning*] Ummmm.

WOMAN: And we discovered we were the ones we had been seeking in everyone else.

MAN: [*gasping in agony*] Owwwww.

WOMAN: We were what we had been looking for.

MAN: [*A death rattle in his throat*] Ahhhh . . . .

[*Immediate blackout*]

INTENTIONAL COINCIDENCE

ACT I
Twins

JERRY: [*Eagerly*] Well hello!
TERRY: [*Wary*] Hello.
JERRY: Fancy seeing you. Here.
TERRY: Where?
JERRY: Here. In the park.
TERRY: Do I know you?
JERRY: I don't think so.
TERRY: Then why were you surprised?
JERRY: Surprised at what?
TERRY: Seeing me.

JERRY: Because I have before.

TERRY: Seen me?

JERRY: Oh yes. Several times.

TERRY: Where?

JERRY: Everywhere. At the school. At the bar. At the bakery shop.

TERRY: You've seen me there?

JERRY: Unless you have a twin.

TERRY: I don't. I don't think so.

JERRY: That's too bad.

TERRY: You like twins?

JERRY: Wouldn't it be nice?

TERRY: I should think it'd be awful.

JERRY: To have someone to love.

TERRY: You don't have to be a twin to have that.

JERRY: Who'd love you very similarly and equally almost back.

TERRY: But what if you fought?

JERRY: You'd know just where to hurt the other one most. But you'd also know he didn't really mean it, that he couldn't really hate you without hating himself.

TERRY: Well I'm not one.

JERRY: One what?

TERRY: A twin!

JERRY: Oh. I'm not one either but I wish I was.

[TERRY *picks up his newspaper.*]

JERRY: You want me to go.

TERRY: It's a public park.

JERRY: Isn't it? [*Confidentially*] A little too public . . . for my taste.

TERRY: Well sometimes it can be very nice.

JERRY: You mean when you're left alone?

TERRY: To read, take in the sun, dream some.

JERRY: What do *you* dream about?

TERRY: I don't think that's your affair!

JERRY: I don't think so either. But you might have bitten!

TERRY: Bitten?

JERRY: Allowed me in . . . just like you did. You see, you don't really want me to leave.

TERRY: I don't?

JERRY: Or you'd just stand up and walk off.

TERRY: But I like this bench.

JERRY: There are others.

TERRY: It's quiet here. Usually.

JERRY: Generally deserted.

TERRY: You know the spot?

JERRY: I've seen you here as well.

TERRY: Well, I've never noticed you.

JERRY: But now you will.

TERRY: Yes. I guess.

JERRY: I noticed you right off.

TERRY: Oh.

JERRY: Aren't you going to ask why?

TERRY: [*Returning to his paper*] No, I'm not.

JERRY: Then I won't tell you.

TERRY: Then don't.

JERRY: And you'll just have to imagine the reason.

TERRY: I like imagining.

JERRY: No you don't. You're a man who acts.

TERRY: [*Putting down the paper*] What makes you say that?

JERRY: I've watched.

TERRY: Watched what?

JERRY: You see? You want to know.

TERRY: Go away!

JERRY: Well then, I won't. [*He sits next to* TERRY.]
[TERRY *moves slightly over.*]

JERRY: [*Moving over also*] You're the one who bites.

TERRY: Leave me alone.

JERRY: I'll tell you why I noticed you.

TERRY: No need to.

JERRY: It's because you're curious.

TERRY: Curious? I'm not.

JERRY: You are. That's why you're everywhere.

TERRY: I hardly ever leave the house.

JERRY: You poke your head in nearly every shop you pass.

TERRY: How do you know that?

JERRY: I've been watching, as I said.

TERRY: [*Really troubled*] Have you been following me?

JERRY: Not exactly.

TERRY: What's that supposed to mean? Have you been following me?

JERRY: Our paths often cross.

TERRY: [*Beginning to stand*] What's this all about?

JERRY: [*Pulling* TERRY *back*] Sit! Sit! I'm not dangerous.

TERRY: Why do our paths cross so much?

JERRY: We must live next door. Or in the very same apartment house.

TERRY: Where do you live?

JERRY: You think I'm going to tell a perfect stranger?

TERRY: I thought you said you knew me?

JERRY: [*Moving closer to him*] Not well enough!

TERRY: [*Sliding away*] Too well for my taste!

JERRY: That's your problem. You don't let anyone close.

TERRY: I have a girlfriend.

JERRY: Not anymore!

TERRY: What do you mean?

JERRY: She's been seeing your other friend, the tall one.

TERRY: David?

JERRY: Yes, the one you like most.

TERRY: What's that supposed to mean?

JERRY: Body language.

TERRY: What are you talking about?

JERRY: You lean toward him. From her you lean back.

TERRY: How do you know he's screwing her?

JERRY: Actually, she's screwing him. She's more interested in another man who I don't think you know. At least I've never seen you with him.

TERRY: You're insane!

JERRY: Probably.

TERRY: You're making this all up!

JERRY: She wore the red parka with this stranger. The one with the yellow dots.

TERRY: An ugly article of clothing!

JERRY: Atrocious!

TERRY: That means you've been following her as well?

JERRY: Yours is not the only path I cross.

TERRY: Are you a spy?

JERRY: Now why would a spy want to waste his

time on you and this David guy and what's her name?

TERRY: Beth.

JERRY: Beth? Beth? What kind of name is that?

TERRY: I always thought it was a nice name.

JERRY: It matches her coat. Now David, that's a *nice* name. Only he cheats. He should have told you all about it.

TERRY: About what?

JERRY: The affair. With Beth.

TERRY: Oh yeh.

JERRY: I knew it. You don't really care.

TERRY: [*Defensively*] I care!

JERRY: No you don't. At least not about Beth. You don't let anyone get too close.

TERRY: I didn't know her very long.

JERRY: Four months!

TERRY: That's not very long.

JERRY: Some people find love in a single afternoon.

TERRY: What do I care? And why am I talking to you about any of this?

JERRY: Because *I* do care. [*Moving closer*] I like to get close.

TERRY: You queer?

JERRY: Yes.

TERRY: [*Doesn't know how to react*] Leave me alone!

JERRY: You're attracted, aren't you? Admit it!

TERRY: I certainly am not!

JERRY: [*Trying to make him laugh*] Just a little bit? A wee bite? A tiny trifle? An infinitesimal wink of the old eyelid?

TERRY: [*Unable not to laugh*] What's your story?

JERRY: My story! You want my story! [*Suddenly standing*] I thought you'd never ask!

THE INCREDIBLE STORY OF ME

When I was one, the age of this first memory, my mother said: I want him dead and put me into the paws of my poor pop, who, not knowing what to do, ran me down to the adoption folks and put me up for auction. I was bought cheaply enough by a couple of busy burghers from the Borough of Bronx, who put me in the capable hands of a teen-age bobbysoxer sitter who undressed and dressed me like a paperdoll all day long in costumes she procured from my drawers and stores at incredible expense: Plucky Little Sailorboy, Sweater-Chested Schoolboy Thug, Velveteen Prig and Sissy, and, one occasion, upon stealing her little sister's britches, Princess with a Terrible Urge to Pee. She took great interest in such things and traveled with me to the potty every hour on the dot. I suffer still from hemorrhoids. And at ten I took off. Not very far. Took myself to the very next block, in response to which my protective parents recognized me as eternally lost. The street is a perfect place for ten-year-olds who want to be picked up and taken home by loving paters. It fit the doll-pattern of my life to that date. But after playing these gentlemen, embarrassed for their retreat to childhood perhaps, break their dolls or toss them into dumps. Like Pinocchio I had to cut the strings and turn into a real boy to get out of there fast. Right into the jaws of justice, the so-called Protectorate of City County State. They sent me to school to learn How to Do It Right. And when I'd gotten it down — and standing up — they released me, spit me up into the very same sures for which I'd swum. But this time I knew what It was all about. At sixteen you get a completely different clientele. As a vision of themselves in the prime of life they invite you back and back — and back like a rear window that looks out over their pasts. The view is better there and you get all the benefits of it: Gonorrhea, Syphilis and such. But back then everything was curable. It gave one a sense of power, of potency. It's hard to face the end of adolescence if that's your act. Ask any High School Prom Queen! or King for that matter. Ask the Captain of the Football Team. Nothing else in life can ever match that! I didn't go to high school. I didn't go to college. I stood there just waiting, waiting for *my* knight.

TERRY: [*Obviously touched*] I didn't know.

JERRY: You like it?

TERRY: I mean, I didn't know it was like that.

JERRY: Did you like it? Did you like the act?

TERRY: What act?

JERRY: [*Sitting down, gently*] You liked it.

TERRY: Was this just an act?

JERRY: [*Putting his hand on* TERRY'S *knee*] You like me.

TERRY: [*Standing in revulsion*] Get away!

JERRY: [*Engagingly*] You like me.

TERRY: Yes. But I hate you. You're disgusting!

JERRY: About what?

TERRY: You play with people. Just like you were talking about! Like they were objects — not beings with real beating hearts.

JERRY: You're right! Like you, I'm afraid.

TERRY: I'm not afraid. If I were afraid I would have left at your very first sentence. You're weird. But I've stayed.

JERRY: [*Smiling to himself*] Yes. But you're scared. I can see you're scared.

TERRY: Of you?

JERRY: Of what I mean, by accosting you like this. By knowing so much.

TERRY: Well yes, I have to admit, it's frightening. You hear about people, people who track down someone they admire or who they are very attracted to . . .

JERRY: Who said I was attracted?

TERRY: Or for whatever reason. Usually it's celebrities, but it could be anyone I guess, who people, people like you, get fixated on.

JERRY: Yes?

TERRY: Well then they . . . . Anything can happen.

JERRY: Love?

TERRY: Murder! Death!

JERRY: What if their victim really fell in love?

TERRY: That's the problem, they're victims. Victims can never really love. They can pretend to. They can imagine they do. But they can never know anything for certain except that they're victims. People without choice.

JERRY: And you equate love with choice?

TERRY: [*Thinking, for a moment stumped*] Yes. Yes I do. There's no real love without your wanting it, your desire.

JERRY: And desire, do we choose that?

TERRY: We can. If we're civilized enough.

JERRY: No wonder you never get close to anyone.

TERRY: Shut up! Just shut up! [*Standing*] What do you know?

JERRY: I don't. I just watch.

TERRY: Well, let me tell you! I loved my father. I loved my mother.

JERRY: That's the most distant love a man can have.

TERRY: Well, I loved them. And as a family we were close.

JERRY: Glad to know.

TERRY: Only one day, I was eight I think, and very educated, quite a bit ahead of my age. I had read all about the Mother Complex and the father, who I never was in conflict with, and the act of sex. And I wanted to see if I would, could possibly have the same reaction as Freud said. I could perfectly well imagine my parents, they were such a handsome couple, having sex. So when I heard groans one afternoon . . . . [*He breaks down.*]

JERRY: You entered their room . . . .

TERRY: Yes. [*Pause*] And there was my father . . . .

JERRY: Fucking.

TERRY: Yes. But it wasn't my mother . . . .

JERRY: [*Sarcastically*] What a relief!

TERRY: . . . but our family pet. A German Shepherd named Frederick.

JERRY: Frederick?

TERRY: Yes.

[*Long pause*]

JERRY: How old were you?

TERRY: Seven. Eight.

JERRY: Already reading Freud?

TERRY: I was advanced.

JERRY: You think maybe it really *was* your mother?

TERRY: Over all these years I've come to presume that.

JERRY: So?

TERRY: But I know it's not so — even if it really is the fact. I saw it . . . I see it still . . . differently.

JERRY: You see, you're just like me. We don't see the world the same as other people.

TERRY: No one does.

JERRY: Exactly!

TERRY: What does all this have to do with us? [*Correcting himself*] With you and your following me. And trapping me today this way.

JERRY: [*Putting his hand on* TERRY'S *knee*] Am I trapping you?

TERRY: [*Leaning back*] Not exactly.

JERRY: [*Rubbing the knee*] No. I've been releasing you. You can go. Anytime you want.

TERRY: I know.

JERRY: But you don't. Want. Do you?

TERRY: Yes! [*Standing*] I must.

JERRY: Yes. I have to cross other people's paths. Here I am spending all this time on you.

TERRY: [*Sitting down again*] Well, I wish you wouldn't.

JERRY: I won't. One often takes wrong paths.

TERRY: Besides, this time I'll recognize you!

JERRY: Yes, and that would take away all the fun.

TERRY: You see, it's you who like to keep a distance between yourself and . . . .

JERRY: The one I like?

TERRY: . . . and anyone.

JERRY: But you're not just anyone. You're the man I recognize from crossing your path.

TERRY: And David and Beth and God knows . . . .

JERRY: Debra, Colette, Carl, Bob.

TERRY: And . . . .

JERRY: Rich. Alan. Carol. Kevin.

TERRY: Do you have conversations with all of them?

JERRY: Oh my jealous one, what does it matter?

TERRY: It doesn't! I mean, it's so strange. You come up to me. You say you know me. Only you don't.

JERRY: I never said I knew you. But now I do.

TERRY: And you know all those people.

JERRY: That's what I mean. I'm just naturally friendly. And you're just naturally not. And I grew up so terribly abused and you so terribly loved. Your father even loved your dog a lot. But you can't find anyone in the whole huge space of this city to even really talk to — but me. Isn't it sad?

TERRY: Yes. In a way. But I'll find someone someday.

JERRY: Perhaps. You found me.

TERRY: *You* found me. But I'm straight.

JERRY: [*Suddenly kissing him square on the mouth*] I know.

TERRY: [JERRY *pulls away;* TERRY *sits, stunned.*] What's your name?

JERRY: Jerry.

TERRY: I know.

JERRY: You do?

TERRY: My name's Terry.

JERRY: Oh?

[*They rise both, and go on their separate ways.*]

ACT II
Facts

BETH: [*Standing next to* JERRY *in the subway*] Hello.

[JERRY *looks around to see who she's talking to.*]

BETH: I said hello.

JERRY: Hello.

BETH: Crowded.

JERRY: Yes.

[BETH *nods her head.*]

JERRY: It always is this time of day.

BETH: I usually take a taxi.

JERRY: They cost too much.

BETH: Yes that's true. That's why I took the subway today.

JERRY: That's why I always do.

BETH: Well, here's my stop. [*She starts to go forward.*]

JERRY: No it's not.

BETH: [*Politely*] How would you know?

JERRY: Yours is 86th.

BETH: Maybe it is maybe it isn't. But maybe I'm going to see someone. Or maybe I work here. Or maybe I just want to shop, see the streets in this neighborhood. But anyway, you're mistaken. I never go up past 72nd.

JERRY: Now you missed this stop.

BETH: I'll get off at the next.

JERRY: I'm sorry.

BETH: What made you say that?

JERRY: I thought I'd seen you. Before today.

BETH: A lot of people look like other people. I have one of those faces.

JERRY: Do you own a red parka, with yellow dots?

BETH: No, I don't.

[JERRY *looks disappointed.*]

BETH: I mean, I did. But it was so tacky, I gave it away.

[JERRY *smiles again.*]

BETH: But a lot of people have those coats. Macy's featured them in '78.

JERRY: That's a long time ago.

BETH: I take special care of my clothing. Besides those were meant to last.

JERRY: Oh, you missed this stop too!

BETH: [*Looking around, a bit confused*] Oh dear, where are we at?

JERRY: Sixty-fifth, Sixty-sixth. I'm not certain.

BETH: You see, I'm going to a play.

JERRY: At Lincoln Center.

BETH: Yes. It's supposed to be just awful, so you don't need tickets.

JERRY: Until you get there.

BETH: Yes. Although I have a friend who some-times, if it's a really empty theater, will let in his friends.

JERRY: For free?

BETH: Yes. Although you have to take him out to dinner.

JERRY: That costs as much as a ticket.

BETH: More. And you have to wait until the play's completely over. And the people have all left. And they've turned out the lights. And the ac-tors have taken off their makeup. And then sometimes they tag along.

JERRY: That sounds like fun.

BETH: But you also pay for them! And they're, in such instances, really not very good. Cause the play bombed. Which is why you were let in.

JERRY: So you pay to see these terrible plays more

than most people pay to see the good ones?

BETH: Yes. So I didn't really want to, I guess.

JERRY: You've *never* been to 86th?

BETH: Well, I used to go there. Years ago. I used to date a guy up that way.

JERRY: Let me guess: Terry? David?

BETH: That's spooky.

JERRY: My having guessed.

BETH: No. I've never dated anyone by either of those names.

JERRY: No?

BETH: But those are the names of my brothers.

JERRY: No!

BETH: Cross my heart.

JERRY: They live there? Up at 86th?

BETH: Oh no. We grew up in Indiana. They stayed.

JERRY: And married?

BETH: In Indiana you don't have a choice.

JERRY: Kids?

BETH: Dozens!

JERRY: Do you ever visit them?

BETH: At Christmas. But I can't stand it. The noise! All that tumult. And the cuteness of everything. I can't wait to get back to the city where, relatively speaking, it's quieter; and it's ugly with grit.

JERRY: You hate pretty things!

BETH: Oh, I don't *hate* them. But a whole room full!

JERRY: I like pretty people.

BETH: So do I! But you know, the people there are really ugly. Fat. Full of wrinkles. Terrible taste. I think that's why they put out so many trinkets.

JERRY: To remind them of beauty?

BETH: No, to distract you from them. Because the landscape, although absolutely boring at first sight, is really beautiful if you look at it right. Silverweeds and black biers in winter, grasses and green leaves all summer long. It's the people and their houses who are the blight. While here all the people and houses are truly lovely while the landscape is all littered up and scratched out.

JERRY: I like pretty people.

BETH: You wouldn't like Indiana much. Because the pretty people leave.

JERRY: And come here.

BETH: Or go to L.A. Have you ever been?

JERRY: Do I look beautiful to you?

BETH: [*Slightly alarmed, she looks over nonetheless.*] No, you don't.

JERRY: Maybe I should go to Indiana.

BETH: Oh, you're not that bad!

JERRY: You belong here. Or even in Los Angeles.

BETH: Thanks. I try to keep fit. I work out at the Episcopalians.

[JERRY *looks confused.*]

BETH: They have a dance program. Modern jazz and aerobics. And you?

JERRY: I drink beer. And watch television a lot.

BETH: [*Laughing, despite herself*] I mean, where did you come from?

JERRY: I thought you'd never ask.

MY LIFE STORY

I was born and raised in Nebraska. I loved the old farmstead. Everyone was lovely: my father, my mother; my sister was Queen of the Prom and State Beauty Pageant finalist. Our dog was sleek and thin. I loved our house. I loved our neighbors. They were beautiful too. But I, I was ugly, a thug. I couldn't cut the mustard. I had to travel East or travel West. But the boys back there and the girls who they wed are sweet and blest.

BETH: You're making fun of me!

JERRY: No, not really. But you remind me of a girl I once knew. By the name of Marybeth.

BETH: [*Startled*] Are you psychic?

JERRY: Why?

BETH: Because my name is Beth.

JERRY: Well, what a coincidence! This was a woman, however, who was city-born and bred and had never set a foot in Indiana or Nebraska or even Missouri. She lived in Manhattan, up on 86th — oh, you've just missed it — well anyway, she doesn't live there today. She married a man from Michigan who liked Lawrence. So they moved out and had a daughter and a son. And now she likes Lawrence too.

BETH: Who's he?

JERRY: An entire city. With lights at night and pretty people and some ugly ones. And murderers and muggers. And lovers so sweet you just have to let them lie in the morning with their backsides to the sun.

BETH: What a strange thing to say!

JERRY: Well, that's what Marybeth used to do when she was dating David up at 88th. You see, I knew David pretty well and he told me what happened to him and her before she left.

BETH: [*Plainly uncomfortable*] Is that what men do? Sit around discussing their conquests?

JERRY: No, I would say the reason he talked about

her was that he couldn't win the one woman over who he loved so much. Oh, he was a wow with others, the blonde secretary types. But Marybeth was a brunette. [*Discovering, as if for the first time,* BETH's *hair, stroking it*] Like you! She was a brunette too!

BETH: [*Quite uneasy*] Well where are we now? I've got to get off!

JERRY: I was just telling you about Lawrence and how mistaken Marybeth had been. Because it really is a very nice place in which to live. And so, I've been told, is Indianapolis.

BETH: I was from Elkhart!

JERRY: Never been there, so I'll have to take your word for it. I live up on 110th. You want to go there?

BETH: Are you trying to pick me up?

JERRY: Just your spirits, dear. Your body, you can leave to Lawrence, Dave and Terry too. But he could have cared less.

BETH: About what?

JERRY: About you.

BETH: The only Terry I know is my brother.

JERRY: In Indiana.

BETH: Well, not anymore.

JERRY: No?

BETH: This summer, when the grass and leaves were as green as they get, he packed a suitcase and snuck out in the deep of one afternoon, leaving his children and wife. No one's heard from him since.

JERRY: I saw him recently in Central Park. He's alright.

BETH: [*Standing*] What are you talking about? Get away from me!

[JERRY *also stands.*]

BETH: Leave me alone! [*She tries to escape but he grabs her.*]

JERRY: I'm not going to hurt you!

BETH: You're mad!

JERRY: I know.

BETH: [*Relaxing a bit*] You're frightening me!

JERRY: [*Letting her go*] I don't mean to. I just have this terrible habit of telling the truth to those who don't want to know.

BETH: But it isn't. The Truth! It isn't. It's just imagination and coincidence.

JERRY: Yes. That's what I mean. Most people just want facts. But I give them something else. I watch. I listen.

BETH: Well, I'm not going to give you any opportunities! [*The car comes to a stop and she turns to* bolt, *asking another subway passenger*] Where are we at?

PASSENGER: 144th Street, The Bronx.

BETH: [*Frightened, turns back*] I've never gone this far before.

JERRY: [*Sitting*] You'll have to go to the end of the line and take it back.

BETH: [*Horrified*] Where to?

JERRY: Back to that terrible play.

BETH: Yes. [*Sitting*] Yes.

JERRY: I bet I can tell you how it ends.

BETH: I can't imagine!

JERRY: With the heroine in possession of all the facts.

[*The train door opens, and he exits.*]

ACT III
The Man in Back

A MAN IN THE CENTER OF A BARROOM: [*Calling over to* THE BARTENDER] I'm in the other room. Tell him. I'm in the back.

[*He exits.*]

JERRY: [*Entering, going up to the bar*] You're new!

BARTENDER: Substitute.

JERRY: Vodka on the rocks.

BARTENDER: You're not a regular.

JERRY: No. I guess not.

BARTENDER: I've been substituting for a few months.

JERRY: I've been away.

BARTENDER: I know.

JERRY: Found another bar.

BARTENDER: Glad to have you back.

JERRY: Glad to be. [*Sips.*] Too high a tone up there!

BARTENDER: Up where?

JERRY: That other place.

BARTENDER: Getting that way everywhere.

JERRY: Where are all the regular folks?

BARTENDER: Plain people? Went out of style.

JERRY: But there's still some drink here.

BARTENDER: Some.

JERRY: Dave come in?

BARTENDER: Dave?

JERRY: Tall guy. Lots of hair. Jet black.

BARTENDER: You mean Terry?

JERRY: No. Terry's blonde. David.

BARTENDER: You mean Terry, that's the one!

JERRY: I'm sure it's David.

BARTENDER: We got a Dave, short, shrimpy guy with glasses.

JERRY: No. This guy's a model type.

BARTENDER: Yep, that's him. Clotheshorse. Man's man. Actor's voice.

JERRY: Yeh.

BARTENDER: Terry.

JERRY: Hmmm. I could have sworn.

BARTENDER: He's in the other room. In the back. Says to tell you that's where he's at.

JERRY: Me?

BARTENDER: Said you'd be coming in.

JERRY: I don't know him. Not really. Just seen him here. About.

BARTENDER: He knows you. Evidently.

JERRY: Described me?

BARTENDER: You're Jerry, right?

JERRY: [Surprised] Yes. But how'd you know?

BARTENDER: That's what he said.

JERRY: He knew my name?

BARTENDER: He's in the back.

JERRY: [Looking around, suspiciously] Well, I'm not here. Understand. I never came in.

BARTENDER: Whatever you want.

JERRY: Another gin.

BARTENDER: [Looks a bit perplexed, but serves it up] Here you go!

JERRY: [Pointing to the back] That's the restaurant?

64

BARTENDER: Yeh.

JERRY: I've never eaten.

BARTENDER: Lamb. Steak. Chops. Mixed grill. Food to chew on.

JERRY: Did he say I was joining him for dinner?

BARTENDER: Nope. Just to tell you where he was.

JERRY: I'm not hungry.

BARTENDER: I've had days like that.

JERRY: I had breakfast. Usually just have coffee.

BARTENDER: Some people eat meat and vegetables and fish and cheese.

JERRY: The Germans.

BARTENDER: [*Disgusted*] Yuh.

JERRY: Lunch is my favorite meal.

BARTENDER: Mine too.

JERRY: Dinner. Now that's too late. You got to sit up with your belly the entire night.

BARTENDER: In France they eat sensibly.

JERRY: In the middle of the day.

BARTENDER: In Spain they eat at ten.

JERRY: Why would he wait in there for me?

BARTENDER: Have to ask him.

JERRY: Good-looking man.

BARTENDER: Ladies love him.

JERRY: You got a wife?

BARTENDER: Women!

JERRY: Neither do I.

BARTENDER: Now Terry, he could have anyone. And there are some lookers who drop in.

JERRY: On the lookout for a man.

BARTENDER: And the men staring back.

JERRY: Like a standoff.

BARTENDER: OK Corral. But Terry never shoots his trap. Just sits there cool.

JERRY: The other guys circle.

BARTENDER: And Terry just waits.

JERRY: And naturally it's him they always want.

BARTENDER: But he never makes a move.

JERRY: And they're too tony to.

BARTENDER: Unless they're whores!

JERRY: Too proud. Too scared. Too uptight.

BARTENDER: So he goes home alone every night.

JERRY: Really?

BARTENDER: Unless he meets them round the corner.

JERRY: I never would have guessed.

BARTENDER: While the other guests, those coarse catcallers who these women — real lookers too — are attempting to ignore begin to get attention. The women fan out, looking over at Terry the entire time, and, one by one, fall into conversation with this accountant, that cop, the truckdriver, who's a slob. While Terry just sits there.

JERRY: Maybe he's married.

BARTENDER: I really doubt it.

JERRY: Why?

BARTENDER: He comes in here every night.

JERRY: Maybe it's an open marriage.

BARTENDER: But he doesn't take advantage. You see?

JERRY: I see.

BARTENDER: If you got something open you got to step into it. Terry just sits it out.

JERRY: Think he's gay?

BARTENDER: Why, if he was, would he frequent this place?

JERRY: You say he said to tell me he was in there?

BARTENDER: Waiting.

JERRY: How long?

BARTENDER: What?

JERRY: How long's he been waiting?

BARTENDER: [*Scoffing*] Well, to be honest, he's been saying that for weeks. Months. Since I been here anyway.

JERRY: No!

BARTENDER: Yep.

JERRY: Waiting for me?

BARTENDER: [*Impatiently*] I told you so.

JERRY: You know, we've never met.

BARTENDER: Really!

JERRY: We've never spoken.

BARTENDER: Whew. That's weird.

JERRY: [*Turning to the room*] Wish I was hungry.

BARTENDER: Maybe you'll work up to it.

JERRY: [*Putting on his coat*] You won't tell him I was here?

BARTENDER: What's it to me?

JERRY: I just got to go.

BARTENDER: I know.

JERRY: This whole thing really amazes me.

BARTENDER: Me too!

JERRY: I mean, why? [*Turning to go*]

BARTENDER: I was beginning to wonder if you really existed. And what'd you be like.

JERRY: [*Turning back*] And what am I like?

BARTENDER: You're real nice.

JERRY: You too! [*He exits.*]

> [THE MAN *reenters the room from the back. He has red hair.*]

THE MAN IN BACK: He come in yet? Tell him I'm in the other room.

> [THE BARTENDER, *wiping down the bar, shakes his head yes.*]

A DOG TRIES TO KISS THE SKY

a short play

[*Two men against the sky*]

ALBERT: Hear him?

BOB: What?

ALBERT: Hear?

BOB: Who?

ALBERT: [*Cocking his head*] He's barking.

BOB: [*Cocking his head*] No. I don't hear him.

ALBERT: Hear him now?

BOB: No, I don't.

ALBERT: Far in the distance.

BOB: I'm supposed to have good ears.

ALBERT: Who says?

BOB: I say. My wife.

ALBERT: [*Cocking his head*] Then you hear him?

BOB: [*Cocking his head*] Nope.

ALBERT: Then you don't.

BOB: I can hear a train.

ALBERT: No train.

BOB: In the distance — there — the whistle.

ALBERT: No train in this part of the state.

BOB: Sounds like a train.

ALBERT: No. It sounds like a dog.

BOB: I mean the whistle.

ALBERT: It's a bark.

BOB: What you hear is — evidently. But I'm hearing a whistle — like the whistle of an engine — of a train.

ALBERT: No train.

BOB: Doesn't sound like a siren.

ALBERT: Ah — that's his howl.

BOB: Doesn't sound like a howl.

ALBERT: But that's what it is.

BOB: You've heard this all before?

ALBERT: Every day.

BOB: In the distance?

ALBERT: Far away.

BOB: And it never comes closer?

ALBERT: Not much.

BOB: And you never move closer to it — to him?

ALBERT: Why should I want?

BOB: To find out if it really is a dog.

ALBERT: Oh it's a dog all right.

BOB: Or why he barks or why he howls.

ALBERT: Don't want to know.

BOB: Maybe it would help.

ALBERT: Help what?

BOB: The dog. Maybe it's lonely.

ALBERT: Probably been beat.

BOB: Maybe he's hurt. You could help him.

ALBERT: I don't like dogs.

BOB: I do.

ALBERT: Then I wish you'd hear him too. You could go out and save him or shut him up.

BOB: I don't hear anything.

ALBERT: [*Shouting*] You could go and shut him up.

BOB: Stop shouting!

ALBERT: Do you read lips?

BOB: [*Confused*] No.

ALBERT: How do you know what I'm saying then?

BOB: I'm not deaf.

ALBERT: Then you shouldn't say so.

BOB: I didn't. It was just a figure of speech.

ALBERT: Well do you hear him or don't you?

BOB: I don't hear him, but I hear you.

ALBERT: Well, you're one of the few people who do.

BOB: Do what?

ALBERT: Hear me. Most people turn away.

BOB: Away?

ALBERT: From me.

BOB: Why should they do that?

ALBERT: Because they can't hear.

BOB: You mean the dog?

ALBERT: The dog. And then me, when they turn away.

BOB: They're just confused.

ALBERT: No. They just doubt.

BOB: Well, I have to say . . . .

ALBERT: I know, you doubt me too.

BOB: It's natural. I mean, when one's hearing is perfectly normal — if not exceptional, which is what most people think perfectly normal is all about — and you hear something someone can't it's natural to doubt that you're really hearing this exceptional thing each and every day.

ALBERT: No, they don't doubt me. They doubt the dog.

BOB: Well they may say they doubt the dog, but it's you — your hearing it that is — that's really behind what they say.

ALBERT: Well hell, I'm here. They got eyes.

BOB: They don't doubt your existence, just your ability to hear.

ALBERT: Well, I do.

BOB: What?

ALBERT: Doubt my existence, after they all turn away. It's like I never existed. Just like the dog. And they certainly no longer hear — if they formerly did — what I have to say about anything — the dog, the weather, the time of day. So after all I go off and stay in a little corner of town where no one ever goes much. And I think to myself.

BOB: What is it you think?

ALBERT: I told you, I think he's being beat.

BOB: I mean, what is it you think to yourself?

ALBERT: Oh, like whether or not he's being beat. Or if he deserved it. Or if he's going to stop. Or if I should take a gun and go over to wherever it is he's howling from.

BOB: You don't like dogs.

ALBERT: That's what I said.

BOB: Why don't you like dogs?

ALBERT: [*Pondering it for a moment*] They bark. And howl.

BOB: Well I know some who don't. Most don't howl. And some don't bark much.

ALBERT: Only takes one.

BOB: Do you hear other dogs?

ALBERT: Of course! All around town.

BOB: Now?

ALBERT: You hear 'em?

BOB: No.

ALBERT: Then why do you expect me to. I'm no better than you up close. When they bark most everyone hears. And that's why they get shut up! But this — he's different. No one hears him — so it appears — but me. So no one — except maybe the man who beats him — cares whether he howls or not.

BOB: Does he ever stop?

ALBERT: [*Looking with disbelief*] Of course! He's gotta sleep. He's gotta eat. I live my life around those few hours. When he sleeps, I sleep. When he eats, I take a quick bite. And once in a while, for a whole day, he sulks. And I perk up and behave — according to the folks hereabouts — like a normal human being. I live in fear of those days. Get all on edge. It's almost a relief when he goes into his yaps again.

BOB: Have you seen a doctor?

ALBERT: [*Pointing in the direction of the hotel*] He's right over there.

BOB: No I mean, have you gone to one?

ALBERT: He's the only one.

BOB: Have you gone to him then?

ALBERT: What for?

BOB: Well, perhaps he could give you something.

ALBERT: Nope. I tried cotton. I tried muffs.

BOB: I mean for your nerves.

ALBERT: My nerves? I'm not nervous. It's you who's nervous. It's the other folks. Nervous about me and about the dog who they can't hear.

BOB: You mean, you don't mind it?

ALBERT: What do you think I've been telling you? Of course I mind it! I detest it! I want to kill the mangy hound. But that has nothing to do with nerves at all.

BOB: It'd sure make me nervous.

ALBERT: What's there to be nervous about? He won't come any closer.

BOB: I mean the constant noise.

ALBERT: There's always lots of noise. There are clouds and the corn, and naturally the people.

BOB: Well, the people yes! But the corn? You mean the wind in the corn.

ALBERT: No, I mean the corn itself. I mean the clouds on a still night.

BOB: I don't think most people hear that either.

ALBERT: Some do. I met a man once who said he could tell you just from careful listening whether it was June or July in a field of corn.

In June the corn just squeals, while in July it crackles like a blanket on a dry hot night. Someone once explained to me the difference between a cumulus and a stratus cloud. A cumulus got a high-pitched little effeminate voice that stutters to the stars, while a stratus got a flat uninflected pitch like a Midway carney Kansasan crying "Come on come on come on in." But no one hears this dog.

BOB: I don't know what else to suggest. Have you ever thought of moving away?

ALBERT: This is where I live.

BOB: I know. But there are lots of other wonderful places to live in. Without dogs in the distance.

ALBERT: I don't think so!

BOB: Just a vacation?

ALBERT: Besides, it might be worse. Another dog might growl or drool or hiss. And I'd miss him.

BOB: Who?

ALBERT: The one who barks. The one who howls.

BOB: I think you've got a problem!

ALBERT: That's what I've been telling you.

BOB: [*Turning away*] What was that?

ALBERT: I know, it's time for you to go. They all eventually turn away.

BOB: I mean that noise?

ALBERT: [*Cocking his head*] That's him!

BOB: He sounds so sad.

ALBERT: Doesn't he?

BOB: Actually he sounds sort of happy.

ALBERT: You think so?

BOB: Sort of silly. Like he's lolling on the lawn with his tongue hanging out.

ALBERT: Could be.

BOB: Whining. No whinnying actually.

ALBERT: It's possible.

BOB: Sort of gurgling low in his throat. Growling now. Hear him?

ALBERT: [*Cocking his head*] Not my dog.

BOB: No?

ALBERT: Nope. Mine barks. Mine howls.

BOB: [*Listening closely*] Mine has gotten very quiet.

ALBERT: Mine hasn't let up.

BOB: Mine has put his head down beside his bowl to drowse.

ALBERT: My dog — the way he howls sounds almost as if he was trying to kiss the sky. Like he was in love with that old cumulus queer.

BOB: I think you've got a great imagination.

ALBERT: You were the one just making it up!

BOB: Yes. But I was trying to show you what you say seems like to others.

ALBERT: That's the problem. They don't got good
ears.
[*In the distance a dog barks, howls.*]
[BOB *shakes his head.*]

FLYING DOWN TO CAIRO

a musical

CHARACTERS
COWBOY a handsome stud
STEWARDESS a male in drag
STEWARD a gay boy
HIGH SOCIETY MATRON a male in drag
THE MONOPOLY MAN woman in drag
DIRECTOR director of the Play

SCENE
The kitchen of the COWBOY'S *ranchhouse and an airplane of the future.*

NOTE: *although most of the characters are in drag, it is very important that this fact is not accentuated, nor should the play be done as camp. Except at the end, where the masks are broken, it would be best if the drag performances were completely convincing. In all art, illusion is crucial.*

ACT I

COWBOY: Wooeee! [*Standing*] Yep! Hey!

STEWARDESS: [*Entering the room*] May I help you sir? [*Putting him back into his chair*]

COWBOY: [*Rising again*] Wooeee!

STEWARDESS: Sir, would you like a magazine?

COWBOY: Fuck no!

STEWARDESS: Sir, if you could just sit, we could take off. It's regulations.

COWBOY: [*Confused*] Take off? Where to? Isn't this a kitchen?

STEWARDESS: Yes sir, it is. But the Captain says you have to buckle up!

COWBOY: What Captain?

STEWARDESS: [*She points heavenward.*]

COWBOY: [*Looking around him*] And where the fuck's my seat belt? [*Standing*] Wooooeeee!

STEWARDESS: [*Pushing him down into the chair again, she takes a tassel down from the curtain and ties it around him tight*] There! What would you like to drink?

COWBOY: [*Trying to undo the rope*] Hey!

STEWARDESS: Vodka? Bloody Mary? Whisky? Bourbon?

[*To each of these* COWBOY *shakes his head no.*]

STEWARDESS: Budweiser?

COWBOY: Yes . . . I guess. But I don't want anything. I'm just happy. I want to celebrate.

STEWARDESS: Well, sir, may I suggest . . . you wait!

COWBOY: Wait?

STEWARDESS: Until we land.

COWBOY: Land? I don't wanna wait. This is my house and if I want to celebrate I can celebrate. Land?!!!

STEWARDESS: Please sir! I have others to attend to. You just behave!

COWBOY: This is *my* house!

STEWARDESS: I'm afraid, sir, you've made a mistake. Everyone knows Cowboys don't have houses. Horses! That's your mistake. You need R before S. That's the rule.

COWBOY: What are you talking about? U *needs* R not *need*. Didn't you ever study grammar?

STEWARDESS: Yes, sir. I'm educated.

COWBOY: And what about ranches?

STEWARDESS: What?

COWBOY: Ranches have houses. Ranch houses! And how could it take off? Tell me. How could *it* take off?

STEWARDESS: I'm sorry, sir, I don't have answers. I just instruct.

[COWBOY *trying to release himself, he takes the chair with him as he stands*]

STEWARDESS: Sir!! [*calling*] Steward! Steward!

[THE STEWARD *appears*]

STEWARD: Sir, sit down!

COWBOY: Hell if I do! [*Sits.*]

STEWARD: Now what seems to be the problem here?

COWBOY: There ain't no problem *here*! It's her . . . and you.

STEWARD: Please sir, just remain seated. We'll be there in just a few more hours.

COWBOY: Where?

STEWARD and STEWARDESS: [*Laughing*] Where? Where? [*collecting themselves*] We don't know yet.

STEWARD: I'm sorry sir, but you must have been sleeping and got confused when you woke up.

COWBOY: I wasn't sleeping. I was just sitting here. I was happy. I wasn't going anywhere
    [*sung as a torch song*]
    I was happy
    simply happy
    happy as a tapi
    oca pudding or a pie.

I was joyful
genuinely joyful
joyful as a truffle
in a snorting pig's eye.

I was pleased
pretty pleased
pleased as the geese
flapping 'cross the sky.

I was tickled
truly tickled
tickled I'd got pickled
from my gin and rye.

Couldn't stifle
my old rifle
aimed the rifle a trifle
bit too high

Killed the goose
the golden goose.
So put my head into
a noose to die.

STEWARDESS: I too am sorry I laughed. It's always distressing to wake up in a strange place and forget who you are and how you got there and where you were just before you got to where you now are.

STEWARD: [*To* THE STEWARDESS] I'll take care of this. [THE STEWARDESS *disappears.*]

   [STEWARD *falls to his knees beside the completely perplexed* COWBOY *and strokes his head.*] Now. Now.

COWBOY: [*Trying to shake* THE STEWARD *off*] Git your fucking hands . . . .

STEWARD: [*Continuing to stroke*] Now. Now.

   [COWBOY *attempts to stand, but is strangely constrained.*]

STEWARD: Now. Now. Be still. Be good. Go to sleep. Here [*reaching over to turn out the lamp upon the table*] I'll turn out the light.

COWBOY: I don't want the light out.

STEWARD: Sure you do!

COWBOY: No, I don't.

STEWARD: [*Stroking his head and allowing his hand to slip to* COWBOY'S *shoulder*] Now be still. It's a long flight . . . .

COWBOY: [*Getting drowsy*] Let me . . . .

STEWARD: [*Quickly dragging his hand across* COWBOY'S *chest*] Go to sleep. We'll soon have a movie.

   [THE COWBOY *falls asleep.*]

STEWARD: Right out of movie!
   Right out of play!

There he is in person!
This must be my day.

[*He dances.*]

Right out of a picture
Adonis brought to birth!
Handsome and so lean
It takes my breath away!

[*He dances.*]

Right off the screen!
Where he's going to stay!
Heaven brought to earth!
Mix of myth and clay!

Right out of movie!
I'm going to make him pay!
So mean, I want to curse him
For not being gay.

[THE STEWARD *dances forward and pulls down a large screen, upon which a movie is projected. In the movie,* THE STEWARD *stands simply in front of a backdrop and speaks directly to the audience.*]

STEWARD IN THE MOVIE: Good evening. I am here to explain the play. To give it a perspective at least. I am in the future [*pointing upwards*] and the Cowboy — with his nostalgia for the late 18th and 19th century agrarian culture and individualistic Romantic cult colored by Victorian platitudes of Good and Evil, Great and Tall, Albert Hall, and Black and White, made hackneyed by the countless motion picture legends which put him, improperly, upon a stallion's rump and into the heroine's sack — lives in the past [*pointing downwards*]. [*Pointing to the audience*] You are in the present. How do *you* expect to understand? [THE STEWARDESS *comes out behind him and puts her hand upon his groin. He slaps it.*] I could explain it — how trite! In the future, as you may have read, the planes are very wide-bodied and contain whole rooms, movie theaters, [*pointing*] tables, chairs, lamps, fireplaces — if you pay enough. [THE STEWARDESS *again touches; he slaps.*] Whole theatres can fit within the confines of a single airline: The Royale, The Lyceum, the Martin Beck — all gone now. You . . . too. The Cowboy never existed. [*He snaps his fingers and the screen snaps up. It is a futuristic airplane that looks like a bar with groupings of heavily padded chairs, 3 or 4 grand tables. A lounge bar appears stage right at which* THE STEWARDESS *and* STEWARD *stand.*]

STEWARDESS: Drink up gentlemen [*looking to the one woman in the group*] and Ma'am!

[*The house lights go up and ushers or actors as ushers or ushers who want to be actors rush forth to offer the audience whatever they want. Drinks, popcorn — no cigarettes!*]

USHERS: [*Down the aisles*] Vodka? Bloody Marys? Whisky? Gin? [*If a member of the audience responds, they immediately deliver.*]

USHER: [*To a man attempting to rise*] Please be seated! We're about to take off! [*The man is forced into his seat. His wife complains.*]

WIFE: This isn't an airplane!

USHER: And you're not an actress! Please sit.

STEWARD: [*From behind the bar, to the audience*] You see, you don't exist. I mean you do. But not in this play. And that's the problem, generally, of every play. Being in the present is so difficult. You're too complex. The theater needs types. The future needs theater. The past needs airplanes to get it to where it never was.

COWBOY: [*At one of the tables, awakens*] Stewardess! Steward! Stewardess!

STEWARDESS: Yes sir, may I help you? I'm at your service. That's my role. To serve you. Want me on all fours?

COWBOY: [*Shocked*] No!

STEWARDESS: I would have said, I can't do that sir. And I'd have been very, very polite. But authoritative, nonetheless. No, sir, that's against regulations, I would have said. But then, later, I would have gotten down doggy style — when everyone was sleeping or pretending to at least.

COWBOY: Where am I?

HIGH SOCIETY MATRON: You're in a very, very boring play.

COWBOY: I'm in what? Who are you?

HIGH SOCIETY MATRON: I'm a High Society Matron. And I find all plays very, very boring — and elucidating too. Which is why I attend the theater — and take him [*she punches her husband, who is* THE MONOPOLY MAN].

THE MONOPOLY MAN: [*Awakening*] Uhhhh. What. Very good! Jolly good! [*Applauding*] That was marvelous.

HIGH SOCIETY MATRON: But there is no more theater. Which is why we fly! On airlines.

[COWBOY *attempts to stand.*]

HIGH SOCIETY MATRON: Which is why [*hitting her husband again*] . . . he drinks.

THE MONOPOLY MAN: Uhhh? Huh? Huh? [*He applauds.*]

COWBOY: You're all crazy!

STEWARD: [*Leaning over the bar*] Nope. It just looks that way from where you're at. You're a different context. Someone else's dream. But that's the way life really is. Only art pretends it isn't.

HIGH SOCIETY MATRON: [*breaking into song*]

I know how strange things
look to normal folk
like you whose springs
aren't wired to unglue
whenever people poke
fun at absolutely no one
but you know nonetheless
who it's directed to
or at and go flying
like a bat about the loony
bin you're not really in
but feel as if you've
been and can't escape this
unpleasant place.

We survive. We survive through art.

I know how odd it seems
to steady souls who never
feel as if they're always
unreal and ever on alert

89

reel in the slightest wake
of other people's passing
by and are not hurt as if they were
about to be criticized by God
for not having died
and living in such fear wear
faces so horrified by traces
of their reported lives
they sadly wish they hadn't
had to bear or take.

We survive. We survive through art.

COWBOY: Art! Now there's something . . . something I comprehend. The air in the early morning purple it's so fresh! Like a good sneeze in the ash left by the fire that kept the coyote off. And the bears! You can nearly smell their hair. The horses have reared, but been safe beside the soft down of bed which encase the legs by which, day after day, they're embraced.

Then there's the sun. The sun first at the earliest instant in which you can see and second, when it's certain in the sky and strong so it hurts your eyes. That's noon and later setting, six, seven in the summer, eight in late July. The bugs bite. And you know it's time to put the steers into circles and center them in. I love the moon and fire and flames lapping at a jack rabbit or some quail you've shot at during the day.

STEWARD: That's real nice. Said pretty too and spoke as best as someone can speak of such things. But it isn't art. Art is something you can't really say, or, if you do, you don't remember that you did or wish you never had if, you remember only part of it, which you never would if it was really true and not what art is.

STEWARDESS: Love is never . . . .

STEWARD: [*Waving her away*] We're not talking about love . . . we're talking . . . talking . . . about art.

STEWARDESS: Isn't that love?

HIGH SOCIETY MATRON: Yes that's love! [*Yawning*] Whatever love is.

COWBOY: No. No. [*Getting excited*] Whoeee! Now I remember. I was going to get married.

STEWARDESS: [*Disappointed*] That's impossible. Cowboys don't get married.

STEWARD: She's right. Cowboys stay single. They live in the bunk house — with other cowboys. A married man is a rancher.

COWBOY: I live in a ranchhouse! And I was . . . going to marry. I remember that much!

STEWARD and STEWARDESS together: Impossible!
[*Vamp.* STEWARD *and* STEWARDESS *begin a striptease, singing as they do so.*]

You can't get married
Without being buried.
It's not in the stars!

You can't be wedded.
It's not where you're headed.
Your genes create the bars.

Cancel your love life.
Don't count on a wife.
Put out your fires.

You can't be happy
By being a pappy.
You're totally ours.

So don't get homey
with matrimony.
You're under *our* powers.

[STEWARD, *in his underwear, claps his hands together. The stage workers rearrange the set to the original table of* THE COWBOY'S *house.* THE COWBOY *sits at the table, his feet, enshrined in cowboy boots, propped up as he reads the paper.*

THE HIGH SOCIETY MATRON *enters, draped in furs.*]

HIGH SOCIETY MATRON: Good morning, darling.

COWBOY: [*From behind the paper*] Mornin'.

HIGH SOCIETY MATRON: Darling?

[COWBOY *ignores her. She taps the side of her glass.*]

HIGH SOCIETY MATRON: Darling! Feet off the table!

[COWBOY *dutifully removes his feet.*]

HIGH SOCIETY MATRON: That's better. Incidentally [*marmaladizing her toast*] I lunched with Marie Billingslea yesterday. Delightful woman, just filled up to her chins with gossip and gab. She says there will soon be an opening.

COWBOY: [*Laying aside the paper*] Opening?

HIGH SOCIETY MATRON: You know. On the Kent & Kent & Kent & Billingslea board. I told her you'd be perfect. She hinted as much.

COWBOY: What's a board?

HIGH SOCIETY MATRON: You know dear. The men who make decisions. All you have to do is meet.

COWBOY: Meet who?

HIGH SOCIETY MATRON: Whom dear. Each other. And you're paid for it.

COWBOY: For what?

HIGH SOCIETY MATRON: For meeting, love. And saying yes or no mostly maybe or it's possible.

COWBOY: [*Going back to his paper*] What are you talking about?

[HIGH SOCIETY MATRON *tingles for more jam.*]

HIGH SOCIETY MATRON: How are the stocks?

COWBOY: What stocks?

HIGH SOCIETY MATRON: *Those* stocks! [*Pointing at the paper.*]

COWBOY: [*Putting down the paper*] Livestock?

HIGH SOCIETY MATRON: No dear. The ones *there*!

COWBOY: Where?

HIGH SOCIETY MATRON: [*Becoming impatient*] In the paper!

COWBOY: [*Confused*] I'm reading the funnies.

HIGH SOCIETY MATRON: The funnies? O dear. [*Putting down her toast and knife.*] You've got to get a hold on yourself. You've got to start memorizing things like the names of bonds and the birthday of the President of the Bank. It's crucial.

COWBOY: For what?

HIGH SOCIETY MATRON: For getting ahead.

COWBOY: You never ride ahead of the herd.

HIGH SOCIETY MATRON: But you have to.

COWBOY: Can't be done.

HIGH SOCIETY MATRON: I'm afraid it must. If you're going to support me in the style I'm accustomed to. In order to keep up the payments for the house.

COWBOY: The house is paid for.

HIGH SOCIETY MATRON: Oh no, dear. I'm afraid it never is.

COWBOY: I built it myself! [*Standing.*]

HIGH SOCIETY MATRON: [*Aghast*] That's another thing we've got to talk about.

COWBOY: You're crazy!

HIGH SOCIETY MATRON: *I'm* crazy! [*Recalling her previous role*] Perhaps a little.

> [*Reprise*]
> I can imagine how unusual
> it must be for anybody who
> is not unusual in the least
> to see a beast in a person
> when just trying to be nice
> turns you to ice since
> you're sure her purr was certainly
> a growl you turn to howl
> and wish her in a coffin
> as often as she says hello

95

> simply feeling mellow
> for her fellows when you
> feel so rotten and forgotten.

> We survive. We survive through art.

But my dear, you're truly dangerous. Going about admitting all these manual things to everyone! It's absolutely embarrassing. Builders build things, not hubbys. Hubbys go to offices and eat too much.

COWBOY: [*Disgusted*] I'm going to work! [*He exits*]

HIGH SOCIETY MATRON: [*Calling after*] Remember dear, tonight is opera night.

> [*Lights out. When they come up again we are in the futuristic airplane.*]

STEWARD: [*Still in his underpants*] You see! Marriage doesn't suit you, does it?

COWBOY: My girl is different. She's gorgeous for one. She's shapelier too. She's a blonde!

HIGH SOCIETY MATRON: [*Offended*] Well!

COWBOY: And she doesn't wear furs!

STEWARD: You don't seem to comprehend. [*He pulls down the movie screen.*] Today's movie is entitled *The Cowboy and the Hen*.

> [*The movie is silent with subtitles, accompanied by organ music.* THE COWBOY *is at table, boots*

upon it, as in the previous scene. THE STEWARDESS, *hair in curlers, dressed in a floral housecoat, is at the stove. She turns to the table, frowns and silently shouts.*

SUBTITLE: You pig! You pig! Get your feet off the table!

COWBOY *dutifully takes his feet from the table and attempts to keep reading.* THE STEWARDESS *places eggs from a skillet onto a plate, and disapprovingly places them in front of* THE COWBOY *who, behind the paper, seems ignorant of their existence.* STEWARDESS *frowns.*

SUBTITLE: Ignoring me again!

THE COWBOY *continues to read.* THE STEWARDESS *turns back to the stove.*

SUBTITLE: You're letting them get cold!

THE COWBOY *puts up his feet again, sliding the plate over with his toe. Close-up of* STEWARDESS *in all her morning fury.*

SUBTITLE: Pig! Nothing but a pig!
A big sow cowering
round the kitchen
for whom I'm itchin'
since nothing's left
save but to dig a grave
and heft into.

She picks up the skillet and hits him over the head. COWBOY *drops the paper and cowers, hands over head, for a moment before he stands and rushes out.* STEWARDESS *picks up his brief case and throws it through the door after him.*

  SUBTITLE: [*The baby cries*] Ahh ahhh ahhh.
STEWARDESS *rushes to rescue it.*
The End]
[STEWARD *lifts the screen.*]

STEWARDESS: You see, you don't make a good husband. Not even for me. [*Pause. Bends to him.*] But we can have affairs.

COWBOY: [*Drawing away from her*] I don't want an affair!

STEWARD: I don't blame you! Male relationships are better. We understand one another. [*He winks.*]

COWBOY: I don't want a relationship!

STEWARD: That's what I've been telling you, you're that type!

COWBOY: I'm not a type!

STEWARD: Oh, but you are. Characters are always types. The playwright can't be expected to include everything. After all, he's only got an hour or two to do it in.

COWBOY: I'm not in a play!

[*The other characters titter.* HIGH SOCIETY MATRON *punches* THE MONOPOLY MAN *awake; he applauds.*]

COWBOY: I'm not in an airplane!

HIGH SOCIETY MATRON: We know that dear. [*Pointing to the audience*] Even *they* know that. But you've got to pretend.

COWBOY: I don't want to pretend. I want to stay at my table in my house and get married! [*Standing*] And I'm tired of being told what I can do or can't!

STEWARD: [*Calling offstage*] We've got a problem! [*No one responds.*] We've got a problem here!

[COWBOY *tries to exit but* THE MONOPOLY MAN *with* THE STEWARD *restrain him.*]

STEWARDESS: You can't just walk off!

[THE DIRECTOR *enters, clipboard in hand.*]

DIRECTOR: What's the problem? What's the problem?

STEWARD: He refuses to play along.

DIRECTOR: [*Checking his script*] He's not *supposed* to play along. That's his role. The rugged individualist.

STEWARD: But he's threatening to walk off!

DIRECTOR: [*Checking his script*] It's just a threat. If he walks, he doesn't get paid. He knows that.

COWBOY: I don't know anything!

HIGH SOCIETY MATRON: You can say that again!

COWBOY: I've got to get out of this place!

DIRECTOR: So do I. If I stay it gets too Pirandelloesque! [*He exits.*]

> [STEWARDESS *comes up behind the restrained* COWBOY *and hits him over the head with skillet from the movie.* THE COWBOY *drops.*]

STEWARDESS: I found it in props!

THE MONOPOLY MAN: Now what will we do? Our hero's gone!

STEWARD: Just sit down, sir. [*To* THE STEWARDESS] You take care of the others. [*Straddling* THE COWBOY] I'll resuscitate *him*! [*He gently pats* THE COWBOY'S *back.*] Wake up, boy. Come on. [*He cannot resist running his hand across* THE COWBOY'S *chest.*] My, you're a broad-breasted man! Come, get up! [*But* THE COWBOY *stays, passed out.*] Oh, dear.

> [*In the background we hear* THE STEWARDESS *offering "Vodka? Whiskey? Beer? Gin?" to the other passengers.* THE STEWARD *abandons his attempt to awaken* THE COWBOY *and begins to undress him instead.*]

> [*In the audience* USHERS *offer "Vodka? Whiskey? Beer? Gin?"*]

STEWARD: Lights! [*Lights up in audience; stage black-out.*]

ACT II

[*Music. In a chair at table* THE STEWARD *sits dressed as* THE COWBOY. *He is completely unconvincing.*]

STEWARD: [*Pretending to awaken*] I must have been sleeping. What a strange dream. [*Shakes his head.*] Whoooeee! Whoooeee! I'm getting married today!

[THE MONOPOLY MAN *enters, cigar in his mouth.*]

STEWARD: What are *you* doing here?

THE MONOPOLY MAN: We need to have a talk, just man to man. [*He sits.*]

STEWARD: How did you get in?

THE MONOPOLY MAN: [*Ignoring the question*] Now this is getting a little tiresome. My wife is a little more bored than usual. And part of the audience, as you can see, has left. You've got to get these ideas about wives and horses out of your head. I know it's disappointing. I know you'd like to have the things that most men do . . . .

STEWARD: [*Out of character for a moment*] Not necessarily . . . .

THE MONOPOLY MAN: That's not cricket! It's not in the script!

STEWARD: [*Returning to his role*] Sorry.

THE MONOPOLY MAN: [*Clearing his throat*] But Cowboys just don't get to do those things. It's the way the old ball bounces. Fate hands each of us a different deck. But you got to play the hand through nonetheless.

> It's just the way it is
> And can be nothing more
> Than the way it will be
> Which will be what it was
> Before after all the key's
> So few of us are free
> To do more than what does
> Get done and wait to see
> What none of us can know
> where we've been
> That it was there we'd go.

[*Confidentially*] Besides, in this second act the airplane's going to be highjacked by Arabs. And we need you to save us! So there. Sorry I had to be so blunt.

STEWARD: [*Sits stunned for a moment*] Arabs?

THE MONOPOLY MAN: [*Going through the cupboards*] IRA. Communists. I forget. You got any port?

STEWARD: Port? No! Lone Star Beer.

THE MONOPOLY MAN: Sounds dreadful. [*Pulling out a cigar*] You want a cigar?

STEWARD: I chew.

THE MONOPOLY MAN: You cowboys certainly *do* have bad habits. [*He exits.*]

>[*The set returns to the futuristic airplane. Behind the bar they have propped up* THE COWBOY, *still comatose, who is dressed in* THE STEWARD'S *costume, which, in the arms and legs, is too short.*]

HIGH SOCIETY MATRON: Steward! Steward!

STEWARDESS: [*Quickly coming forward*] May I help? The Steward is busy at the moment.

HIGH SOCIETY MATRON: [*Peeved*] What time do we land?

STEWARDESS: Oh dear. We never land. Didn't they tell you that?

HIGH SOCIETY MATRON: Good heavens, no! No landing? What kind of flight is this?

>[THE COWBOY *awakens, holding his head. He*

quickly observes his costume, and looks confusedly about. Pause.]

DIRECTOR: [*From off stage*] Repeat the last line, High Society Matron.

HIGH SOCIETY MATRON: [*Peeved*] What kind of flight is this?

    [*Beat.*]

THE MONOPOLY MAN: [*To* COWBOY] Your cue, old boy.

COWBOY: [*Playing* THE STEWARD] As you may have guessed, this voyage is a metaphor for many things: the search for identity and for meaning, a voyage of desire and longing; a voyage of life . . . and death.

HIGH SOCIETY MATRON: Oh dear!

STEWARD: That was terrible! I want my costume back.

COWBOY: [*Coming over to him*] Now sir, just sit down! [*Relishing his newfound power, he puts his hands on* THE STEWARD's *head.*] Just sit back! You're disturbing the other passengers.

STEWARD: [*Trying to rise*] Now see here!

COWBOY: Stewardess, do you still have that skillet?

STEWARDESS: Oh yes, sir, I still do.

COWBOY: I may have to use it.

104

STEWARDESS: Oh, I'll do it! It's the most power I've ever had over anything in my life!

COWBOY: Just keep it handy.

STEWARD: Okay. Okay. I'll be still. Stewardess, may I have a magazine?

STEWARDESS: Certainly sir. But wouldn't you prefer to go to sleep?

STEWARD: No, I most certainly would not! I'm not supposed to be here.

STEWARDESS: Buckle your seat belt, sir, we may have some rough times up ahead!

[*While this scene has played,* THE HIGH SOCIETY MATRON *and* THE MONOPOLY MAN *have gone into the corner to disguise themselves in strange costumes, wigs and masks.*]

COWBOY: Over to the right you'll observe the Great Windy City of Chicago and to the left . . . .

THE MONOPOLY MAN: [*Brandishing a gun*] Everybody over there!

HIGH SOCIETY MATRON: Yes, over. Now! We're desperate!

STEWARDESS: [*Looking to* THE COWBOY *for help*] Oh dear!

COWBOY: Don't look at me. I'm just a steward now. [*He sits.*]

THE MONOPOLY MAN: [*to* THE STEWARDESS] Go

tell the Captain we've got guns and we want
to go to Cairo!

COWBOY: Cairo?

STEWARD: Cairo?

STEWARDESS: Why would anyone want to go to
Cairo?

THE MONOPOLY MAN: I don't know.

HIGH SOCIETY MATRON: But that's where we
want to go.

> Cairo Cairo Flying Down to Cairo
> We just know that we'll be happy there.

> Flying Flying Flying Down to Cairo
> They'll stand up and stare
> At our dash and dare.

> Cairo Cairo Flying Down to Cairo
> We just know that we'll be happy there.

> Flying Flying Flying Down to Cairo
> When we hit hot air
> They'll be no more terror.

> Cairo Cairo Flying Down to Cairo
> We just know that we'll be happy there.

> [*They dance madly*]

> Cairo Cairo Flying Down to Cairo
> We just know that we'll be happy there.

THE MONOPOLY MAN: So shake a leg.

[THE STEWARDESS *goes for the Captain.*]

HIGH SOCIETY MATRON: Now what?

THE MONOPOLY MAN: We wait.

HIGH SOCIETY MATRON: I'm *bored.*

THE MONOPOLY MAN: Then shoot one of the passengers.

HIGH SOCIETY MATRON: There's an idea. [*Pointing her gun at* THE COWBOY] I should shoot him for calling me a frump! But I was married to him? Or was it him [*pointing to* THE STEWARD]? I'm all confused.

THE MONOPOLY MAN: Just remember, you're a highjacker *now.*

HIGH SOCIETY MATRON: Yes! Yes! [*She shoots* THE COWBOY] There, take that!

[THE COWBOY *falls dead. But* THE STEWARD *quickly grabs her and wrestles her to the floor. The gun drops from her hand.* THE MONOPOLY MAN *shoots wildly.* THE STEWARDESS *reenters.*]

STEWARDESS: Oh my God, he's shot out a window!

STEWARD: [*Screaming while reaching for the gun*] Oh my God! We're all going to crash!

[THE STEWARDESS *quickly grabs the gun.*]

STEWARDESS: Eeeekkk! Now everyone just stay put. We're going to fly to . . . Aruba.

COWBOY: [*Half sitting*] Aruba?

STEWARDESS: I've never been to Aruba. I've never been anywhere to tell the truth. I'm always on my way to some place or always coming back. And I'm tired of hawking alcohol and cleaning up dirty dishes.

THE MONOPOLY MAN: May I remind everyone that I still have a gun! And we're about to crash!
[*Everyone screams.*]

STEWARD: [*Jumping upon* THE COWBOY] Oh my darling, they've shot you!

COWBOY: [*Trying to rise*] Off! Off me!

STEWARD: Darling. Oh my darling!

COWBOY: I want my clothes back!

STEWARDESS: Oh God, don't let us crash!
[*Blackout*]

ACT III

[*Lights up. Characters are precisely where they were in the previous scene.*]

THE MONOPOLY MAN: That certainly was a short break!

STEWARDESS: Why do you supposed they stopped the action like that? [*Remembering*] Eeeekkkk! We're about to crash.

STEWARD: [*Standing, with a big smile. He is bare-chested*] The action didn't stop. THE COWBOY and I just had wonderful, wonderful sex.

COWBOY: [*Standing, in his jockey shorts*] We did *not*!

STEWARD: Oh yes we did. It's in the plot.

COWBOY: But I'm not!

THE MONOPOLY MAN: I told you what you are. You can't change what you've been dealt by fate.

COWBOY: You didn't tell me anything . . . .

THE MONOPOLY MAN: I told someone.

STEWARDESS: [*To* COWBOY] Now that's your problem. You're so completely naive. You just don't seem to understand. But we've all been trying to tell you and you just refuse to listen and then bellyache. Well, I'm sick of it. You are a pig!

COWBOY: I'm a what?

STEWARDESS: A pig!

COWBOY: So now I'm a pig?

STEWARDESS: To have done it with *him*!

COWBOY: I didn't do anything.

STEWARD: That's what they all say!

COWBOY: Give me back my boots!

STEWARD: [*Stepping out of them*] Here, dear. They almost fit!

COWBOY: Stop calling me that! And you [*pointing at* THE HIGH SOCIETY MATRON] why did you shoot me?

HIGH SOCIETY MATRON: I've never shot a gun before! And you said such very bad things about me. All I wanted was for you to be a success!

COWBOY: I didn't say *anything*! [*Looking around*] You're all a bunch of loonies.

HIGH SOCIETY MATRON: I suppose . . . . [*She is about to launch into another verse of "Crazy"*]

STEWARD: [*Interrupting*] See how he tries to wiggle out of it?

STEWARDESS: Yes, I do, and that's what I'm talking about . . . .

THE MONOPOLY MAN: 'Fraid they got you old man.

STEWARDESS: Bellyache! Deny! Play dumb! You certainly don't have a very large *range*.

COWBOY: Three million acres.

STEWARDESS: [*Ignoring him*] Now look at The Monopoly Man there. Before this role she was a nun in — what was the name of the play, hon?

THE MONOPOLY MAN: *Black Beauty*.

STEWARDESS: *Black Beauty*? Anyway. And she was a masseur on Perry Mason once. And he [*pointing to* THE HIGH SOCIETY MATRON] — sorry sweeheart — was in the Rockettes for a week before they discovered his wig. And he was murderer in a Walt Disney movie once. And I — I've played all sorts of roles — con-men, jockeys, wizards, princesses.

STEWARD: I haven't had as much experience as them, but I was Santa Claus once in Summer Stock! [*Proud of the fact.*]

STEWARDESS: But you can't even play the Cowboy right. Life is strange, and that's what makes it so fascinating — worth living completely through. You get lots of chances to be anything you want to be, but you got to first really be one thing. If you're a Cowboy you got to be a cowboy and then you can marry a Steward if you want. But first you got to completely see the part through.

COWBOY: But what's a cowboy? What's a steward? In real life, they're lots of different things.

STEWARD: That's been my point all along, sweetheart, this isn't life — this is art!

COWBOY: Then what does it mean to them? [*Pointing at the audience*] They live in complexity.

What can they gain from the simple messages we preach?

STEWARD: They don't gain a thing.

HIGH SOCIETY MATRON: That's why plays with messages bore me. But then all plays bore me. And he sleeps through them.

STEWARDESS: Well, I'm sorry I got so preachy, but you angered me.

STEWARD: You just wanted to get into his pants.

STEWARDESS: Yes, I guess we all want to be loved.

[DIRECTOR *enters with a captain's hat on his head.*]

DIRECTOR: I had trouble holding our course, but I think we're spared. Now what's the trouble back here? Who wants to go to Cairo?

THE MONOPOLY MAN and HIGH SOCIETY MATRON: We do!

Flying Flying Flying Down to Cairo
Now we'll get there
Without any airfare.

[*The whole cast joins it.*]

Cairo Cairo Flying Down to Cairo
We just know that we'll be happy there.

DIRECTOR: You have my permission.

STEWARDESS: I want to go to Aruba.

DIRECTOR: I'll take you there. [*To* COWBOY *and* STEWARD] And you two?

STEWARD: We want to be married.

COWBOY: No we don't.

STEWARD: Yes we do.

DIRECTOR: I'm sorry, but I've got to draw the line. I don't marry queers.

STEWARD: Oh, that's alright. He's not queer. He's a Cowboy!

COWBOY: No! I'm not!

DIRECTOR: Okay. Do you Steward take this man to have and to hold in sickness and in health till death do ye part?

STEWARD: Yes!

DIRECTOR: Do you Cowboy take this man to have and to hold in sickness and in health till death do ye part?

COWBOY: [*Confused*] What does the script say?

DIRECTOR: It doesn't. It doesn't say anything.

[*Blackout*]

[*Music*]

THE BUSINESS

ACT I

The act should be played in theatrical lighting surrounded by complete darkness.

JOHN VICTOR HERBERT *and his wife* MRS. H *are in the kitchen of their comfortable little cottage, he at the table, she at the stove.*

JOHN VICTOR HERBERT: Me o my!
MRS. H *pays no attention.*
JOHN VICTOR HERBERT: Oh dear, dear me. O my.
MRS. H *looks at him with a sneer.*
JOHN VICTOR HERBERT *lets out a long sigh.*
MRS. H: What's it you got to say?
HERBERT: Nothing. O my.
MRS. H: Out with it!
HERBERT: What's going to happen to me?
MRS. H: I'm going to bean you!

HERBERT: You're what?

MRS. H: If you don't shut up!

HERBERT: Oh dear!

MRS. H *says nothing.*

HERBERT: O my!

MRS. H *leans forward.*

HERBERT: Oh —

MRS. H: I'm hitting you right over the head as hard as I can, you sigh me or my again!

HERBERT: [*surprised*] Sorry.

MRS. H: Just tell me what the problem is.

HERBERT: Oh nothing.

MRS. H: [*threatening him with the skillet*] Spill the beans! Out with it!

HERBERT: I'm going to be fired.

MRS. H: You *what?*

HERBERT: Fired.

MRS. H: *Were* you?

HERBERT: Going to be.

MRS. H: How do you know?

HERBERT: Oh me. Oh my.

MRS. H: [*skillet up*] What for?

HERBERT: Well I don't really know what for. But I can sense. Oh you can tell!

MRS. H: [*sitting down*] Tell? Who said what?

HERBERT: Nobody said anything.

MRS. H: Come on — out with it!

HERBERT: Maybe I should quit — resign before they do it!

MRS. H: What are we going to live on?

HERBERT: It'd be better than the sack.

MRS. H: John Victor Herbert, I want answers! Now.

HERBERT: Oh dear. That's the problem, isn't it? Everyone does. Mr. Smiley — he wants answers too. But that's the problem — which ones?

MRS. H: Which ones? Answers are answers.

HERBERT: Oh no! Really they're not! If I were to ask you why do you love me, what would you say?

MRS. H: That I don't.

HERBERT: You see what I mean? Now you know and I know you really do — some — love me a little — on better days.

MRS. H: An answer's an answer. And don't try to squirm out of this.

HERBERT: [*shaking his head*] See? You're just like Mr. Smiley. He asks, Mr. Herbert (that's how it talks), Mr. Herbert, come in and sit! Come in here! Mr. Herbert, can we meet in a few minutes? Yes, Mr. Smiley, I say yes. Are you being condescending with me, Mr. Herbert, Mr. Smiley asks. What do you mean, Mr. Smiley, I ask? You know what I mean, Mr. Herbert, Mr. Smiley says! But I don't truly understand so I say, No, I don't truly understand, Mr. Smiley, what you mean by condescending, Mr. Smiley. I truly don't. And he says, You're a yes man, Mr. Herbert, that's the problem with you, Mr. Herbert, a yes man through and through. Which I can't stand, comprehend? Higgins Higgins and Lillian Higgins don't like yes men. You got that Mr. Herbert? Not one little bit. Come in to me in a few minutes — no, right now! I've got to get to the bottom of this. Yes sir. I mean, no sir, but I will if you want me to, unless you don't want me to and want me to say I will instead. Don't get coy with me, Mr. Herbert. I'll not tolerate that. We seek truth. Truth in business is our motto if you remember, Mr. Herbert. Oh yes, sir, I remember, Mr. Smiley, I certainly do, since several years ago, if you remember, Mr. Smiley, before you came here or maybe it was before you came to the 32nd floor, I invented it. Invented? Mr. Smiley huffs. That's down on 27 or 28th! Well then, I say, made it up, coined a phrase so to speak, to Mr. Higgins, the elder Mr. Higgins, before he retired and then, God bless him and Lillian, he had that heart attack. Old age, Mr. Herbert, old age. No attacks were described in the company report. Yes, before he tragically and so unexpectedly died of . . . old age, well I was telling him one night to get a slogan and he said Herbert (that's the way he spoke), Herbert, I've been thinking about that I've been thinking a great deal which as you know is difficult to do when you are as busy a man as I am but — I've been thinking yes I mean that — we ought to have — what did you call it? A slogan I said. Exactly Mr. Higgins repeated exactly. Business is Business with us! What you think, Herbert, what you think? Well Mr. Higgins Business *is* certainly that, I said, it most certainly is . . . .

MRS. H: Skip that, I've heard it two thousand times!

HERBERT: Oh no but it's very important to tell *everything* if you really want an answer that is. But then you probably don't.

MRS. H: I do.

HERBERT: You say that, but so does Mr. Smiley and I can assure you he doesn't really want one. Yes is *more* dangerous.

MRS. H: [*skillet overhead*] Go on!

HERBERT: Well I will. But just remember what you said about really wanting to hear because I found — only recently really — but often — and even in the old days some — people say they want an answer when they don't want one. What to do about starvation for example. Or about poverty. Or about people who live on the street. People are always asking what can we do about these things. And anytime somebody says we should do this or we should do that — have you noticed — people say oh but no that isn't the answer. And then another day they say what can be the answer to these problems. And this goes on and on week after week, month after month, year after year. And people starve. And people are poor. And people sleep on park benches, in bus depots and train stations, and even on the sidewalk.

MRS. H: That's 'cause they think more complexly than you do!

HERBERT: Perhaps. But that's my point. I don't have a simple answer for Mr. Smiley nor do I for you. But you both want it short and simple and so, when I try, against my better judgment to answer your questions you always say, as Mr. Smiley always does, Mister Herbert that won't float. Or you're just a yes man or — and this is *your* voice — you're not really saying anything, when I am trying to.

MRS. H: [*waving him on*] Go ahead!

HERBERT: Now I've forgot.

MRS. H: Business means Business.

HERBERT: [*remembering*] Oh it certainly does! But Mr. Higgins thought that Business *was* Business, only since he was still living it expressed it in the present tense. At Higgins and Higgins — as you know Mrs. Higgins became a partner after his death — Business *is* Business. But I felt that although that was true that it might not express much to the people outside the business community to whom we were trying to sell our products to. Perhaps Mr. Higgins I said at that time — and you'll recall that I was telling this all to Mr. Smiley who is a listener far more impatient than you — perhaps "Business Is Truth." Pardon me said Mr. Higgins, what did you say? As a slogan: At Higgins & Higgins Business is Truth. But it isn't he exploded! Oh I know that Mr. Higgins, I know — I'm not as naive as they think I am or you do . . .

[MRS. H *snorts.*]

HERBERT: . . . but as a slogan. That wouldn't be honest Mr. Higgins argued. You want me to lie? No Mister Higgins. No! But you see since you do *believe* in honesty and truth *personally* perhaps it would be nice to characterize your business as that too. Mister Herbert (and that was the only time I recall him addressing me as Mister) — Are you objecting to my practices Mister Herbert Mr. Smiley interjected? Oh no I was just reporting that since he normally called me plain Herbert I'd gotten rather used to it and was surprised by the sudden formality. You know Mr. Higgins the elder was not normally a formal man . . . .

MRS. H: Will you get to the point?

HERBERT: Oh but I am. I am. Where was I? Yes, he wasn't normally. It surprised me to be addressed as Mister Herbert, you are *not* a business man! But of course I was and I couldn't comprehend since I'd spent practically my whole life in business, first as a clerk, then as a salesman, and as an ad-man after that and had had to make the slogans and direct the campaigns for several of our products why he would say that. So I said Mr. Higgins what ever can you mean? a little bit afraid I must tell you to ask because — you see I'm not stupid despite what you say — it might have been a very cryptic way of saying I'd got the can. Only he laughed and put his arms about me and kissed me on the cheek. What do you think of that!

MRS. H: I think he was an old fucking queer whose balls had been deservedly cut off by Lillian, his wife. Everyone knew she ran the company — even way back then — everyone but you!

HERBERT: He hugged me and kissed me just like they do in France. I'll never forget that! And of course that became the slogan Our Business Is Truth, a very successful slogan too since the IRS has never come down on us like they have on the competition and the FCC has left us pretty much alone. And the FBI likes us I truly think they do with our good American values so ex-emplified in our overwhelming success. So Mr. Smiley I say, you can see I know all about our business and all about our truth.... Are you threatening me he interrupts. Threatening? I ask in absolute confusion. Sounds like black-mail if you ask me he erupts. Blackmail? I blurt back. Whatever can you mean? Don't get coy. Yes Mr. Smiley you've already said that, but what do you mean? I just said I know all about truth ... and our slogan. And I'm not playing coy or being clever or playing the yes man I can assure you. You're contradicting me again

Mr. Herbert, arguing. Mister Herbert you don't seem to understand: We here at Higgins Higgins and Lillian Higgins are one big happy family. And you — you're like some little caviling cousin or an aunt someone left up in the closet for too long. Join us or you're gone!

MRS. H: You're right! For once you're right! They're after your job!

HERBERT: O dear! O my.

MRS. H: Stop blubbering. We've got to plan a strategy. How could you have let yourself get into such a position — and with him! Lillian Higgins' secret lover yet!

HERBERT: Whose secret lover? You've got to be crazy! Mr. Smiley. And Lillian! [He laughs.]

MRS. H: [She shoots a dark glance] Everyone knows that!

HERBERT: She's nearly 87. Mr. Smiley is well I'd guess thirty-two, thirty-three, thirty-six tops! Why'd he want an old bag like that?

MRS. H: Some mature women are appealing to young men. And besides, you fool, it's the money he's interested in.

HERBERT: Then what's he working on the thirty-second floor for when he could have been o I'd think on any floor of his choice?

MRS. H: Just a cover!

HERBERT: Besides I've seen him at the urinal and I'm not saying what he was doing but I can tell you with a certain certainty that is without much doubt he definitely likes men.

MRS. H: What does that have to do with anything? *She* doesn't know that! You're an idiot!

HERBERT: O dear, it's all over then.

MRS. H: What's all over? What?

HERBERT: I mean my job.

MRS. H: [*sniffing something wrong*] Yes! It looks like you're a goner if we can't cook up something quick. How about Junior?

HERBERT: O Sonny — that's his real name if you recall — hasn't been seen since 1958!

MRS. H: A cement swim suit if you ask me — present of his mother or his old fart father.

HERBERT: Whatever do you mean?

MRS. H: Oh shut up! I didn't mean the son, I meant his allies.

HERBERT: Allies?

MRS. H: The ones who hate Lillian.

HERBERT: Well there certainly are a lot of them. Hundreds. Nearly everyone. Except — and this makes me wonder whether maybe you weren't right — you're so perceptive sometimes about all of these things — Mr. Smiley. He has never said anything bad about her. Now and then he will join in a laugh but generally discourages such things.

MRS. H: Why that's it! That's it! How old was Junior?

HERBERT: Sonny! When?

MRS. H: When he disappeared, you dolt!

HERBERT: O gee that's hard to remember, it really is. 1958. That's the year of — the Crawford account . . . .

MRS. H: Oh shut up!

HERBERT: But you remember that?

MRS. H: No. I'm afraid I don't Now get to figuring quick! [*She holds the frying pan again.*]

HERBERT: O sure you do! Mr. Crawford wanted a cow on his logo and came to me to find a name for it. And we really thought since he was the sausage king he ought to use a pig, but Crawford was originally Jewish — now you've got to recall the fuss over that — and absolutely detested swine. He wouldn't even think of it! And I thought and I thought. Elsie was already taken and Bessie was too common and — God forgive me for swearing —

MRS. H: Will you stop!

[HERBERT *stops momentarily in shock.*]

MRS. H: How old was Sonny boy?

HERBERT: [*pausing*] I thought of all the names that might be appropriate for a cow. But none of them appealed to me or Mr. Higgins much. And then you said how about Cynthia?

MRS. H: You're hopeless!

HERBERT: How about Cynthia. You said it standing right over there about a foot away from where you're standing now. I remember it plain as day — How about Cynthia? And it clicked! It just clicked. Cynthia the Cow. It was perfect.

MRS. H: [*furious*] I never said that name in my life! [*She puts a pan of water on the stove and lights it.*]

HERBERT: O but you did. Cynthia. The name I presented to Mr. Crawford the very next morning. If you recall — and I know I must have told you this — Sonny said that's great, absolutely brilliant, and Mr. Crawford started to sputter. I've never seen anyone do anything like that again. He spit, he fumed, he got red and just like a volcano sputtered, erupted right over everyone in that room. [*He's laughing now.*] Seems he was having an affair with a secretary right in our offices by the name — you guessed

126

it! — of Cynthia. There was no way to convince him that none of us knew and hadn't staged this elaborate joke. Of course it cost us the account. And Sonny was demoted having put his foot in his mouth. The Higginses had always had this habit of saying absolutely nothing to the customers about an ad-man's pitch. And then, if a client didn't like what he saw they'd make a big stink and fire the guy right there in front of him. Get your things and get out of here — *now* — Mr. Higgins would bark. So the ad-man would leave for a couple of weeks and come back with a good tan and go back to work again like nothing had happened even though everyone knew it had. But good things came of that mistake. Mr. Crawford went back to his wife and they produced a son, William Junior, who put the pig on the label where the cow was to have been. And the company increased its profits, o I'd say by twenty-two, twenty-three percent.

MRS. H: You see this pot? It's now filled with boiling water about to be poured onto your lap if you don't answer my questions with number — *now*!

HERBERT: [*Opens his mouth.*]

MRS. H: Nothing else!

HERBERT: [*Closes his mouth. Counts on his fingers*]. Eighteen.

MRS. H: [*She counts on her fingers.*] Perfect. Oh it's perfect! [*She hugs her husband, to his complete confusion.*] Just perfect!

HERBERT: [*bemused and delighted*] What's going on?

MRS. H: [*getting serious again*] And no one's seen him since?

HERBERT: That's what they say.

MRS. H: Who says? Who?

HERBERT: Everyone. The secretary to Lillian. In accounting. Even Mr. Ratzinger.

MRS. H: That terrible little man?

HERBERT: Yes, librarian. He was telling me one day . . . .

MRS. H: [*completely interrupting him*] It's wonderful! It's perfect! If no one's seen him since 1958 he can come back! To claim his name in the company. To head it up. Lillian won't have a leg to stand on.

HERBERT: O dear — that's funny it really is!

MRS. H: What's funny? What?

HERBERT: O don't you know — Old Mrs. Higgins has been wheelchair bound for o I'd say two years, three . . . .

MRS. H: It doesn't matter.

HERBERT: Makes it hard on her I'm sure. Such an active type.

MRS. H: Don't you understand what I'm talking about?

HERBERT: [*truly confused*] No. No I don't.

MRS. H: He. Sonny. The Higgins of Higgins and Higgins and. Could be anyone. And they'd have to accept him. They'd gladly take him on. He'd be elected President of the Board! He'd be rich! Oh what a coup!

HERBERT: If he came back . . . yes I guess they'd have to take him on again. Pretty happily too. But not if Lillian did what they say she did. Not if she murdered him. O if the old man had only lived I don't think he would have. I like him. The only time I've been hugged by a man.

MRS. H: Stop mumbling! Don't you understand. She *couldn't* say anything. And it could be anyone . . . .

HERBERT: Perhaps.

MRS. H: Even our son!

HERBERT: But we don't have a son.

MRS. H: [*triumphantly*] Oh yes we do! I've been hiding him from you! Keeping him pure. Not letting your madness influence him. [*She goes to the basement door.*] Son. Sonny come on up. I want you to meet your father.

HERBERT: Son? Sonny? When did this happen?

MRS. H: Why in 1958 of course.

HERBERT: But why? How could you have kept him away from me who loves children so much?

MRS. H: Well now you can prove it. Prove your love! [*Down on her knees, intensely and conspiratorially*] Teach him *everything*.

HERBERT: Teach him? What?

MRS. H: Everything you know.

HERBERT: [*completely dazed*] Everything?

MRS. H: Everything. About business.

[*We see a figure in the open doorway.*]
[*Blackout*]

ACT II

The living room of the Herbert home. Pleasantly appointed. Mrs. Herbert stands with a dust rag in hand. From the other room, the occasional sound of male voices. Soft, yellow light, almost nostalgic.

MRS. H: [*dusting a lamp, a process which all the other furniture in the room undergoes throughout her monologue.*] He's handsome isn't he? A little pale, perhaps. But what do you expect? I had to keep him out of harm's way. His father, as you can see, is a monster. A fool! The village idiot. An utter nincompoop. A ninny, a simpleton! An asshole, oh yes, he's that. You have no idea what I've had to put up with. But you can guess.

So I kept him out of sight. If I had a normal husband, of course, there would have been no way to hide him so completely. But John Victor Herbert is not a normal man. Woodworking in the basement? Never. Tool shop? He's afraid of the dark, of cobwebs, and damp. Fuse needs changing, who do you think the job falls to? I put up peach preserves every August. Tomatoes. Canned corn. Vinegar and onions. Peas. On cereals and dried prunes and nuts I overstock. Taught him at an early age how to fend for himself. There. In that damp, dark, and cobweb-pocked basement; he thrived in the very spot which his father feared even to transgress.

And I taught him things. Whispered him words of advice. Numbers. Names. Catalogues. How to make lists. How to read manuals and what needed to be fixed.

John Victor Herbert wouldn't have taught him that! Words. Words. That's all that man is. Made of them. Millions of them. Trillions. I can't think so high. Tomfoolery. Nincompoopery. *Truth*. Wouldn't know enough even how to knock on the door behind which it lurked. My son knows how to lathe that door, drill, bolt, and lay it in its jamb. He can put the knob on and lock and unlock it. He's got the tools to enter into something and come right back out again without going berserk.

You've got to understand. When I was young I too was romantic. I also believed a bit. Life was going to go somewhere and I was going there with it. We'd eventually go on an Atlantic trip, go to Europe and eat schnitzel (not the way my mother used to make but the *real* thing) and drink a couple beers. We'd see the sunset and whistle, maybe even cross the Seine, the Thames, the Po. I got an B+ in geography when I was young.

But things begin to happen, or worse yet, they just don't. The same things keep happening day after day. Night after night. I used to like canned corn, peas, and tomatoes. Now I don't. Can't stand their sight! But a kid needs vegetables in his diet as well as cereal and nuts. So all August I stand in the kitchen shelling and husking to the boiling bottles' click. You hate it, but you do it. You do it. And you do it. And after awhile you don't even think a thing about doing it all over again. But you haven't crossed the Po or even the street. And you know life shouldn't have been just one big repeat. I hate to dust. [*She dusts.*]

Words. They pile up. Sometimes they're sharp. Sometimes they stick you in the heart. Action is at least clean. You do it and it's over with. Even if you have to do it soon again. At least it takes you across the room and into the basement to a little solace with your son. Words just clutter up the house. You can't eat them. You can't wash and clean them. You can't even dust them off. So after awhile you tend not to believe much in what's said. Who told you life was going to be great? That there'd be places to go, a way to get there and someone to go there with. I don't even believe the Seine exists.

Mr. John Victor Herbert doesn't get it just one little bit. Life is a business. And business *is* business, nothing else. High ideals aren't going to put the carpet on the floor or the lamp on the hearth. And you're not going to be able to hold on to anything long if you don't have a door lock. Leave the door open and the world just comes in, even if you haven't been able to get out to it. It takes away your lamp, your rug — even your life.

My uncle was killed on his very own porch just for a quarter. A tornado took away my aunt. I know it sounds funny but it's true. You have to sit and shell peas for what seems like an eternity and you still might not have anything in the bowl when it's over. Words don't help. If God is such a mystery I wish he'd stop revealing himself.

A door has got to be locked. Every day you have to feed your family. Shell the peas, husk the corn. Dust and dust and dust. And at the end of the day you've gotten no further than the other side of the room or down to the basement for a bit. That's life. That's life's business. Being lived out over and over again each day. You can go to church on Sunday and the Thames for a week; but it doesn't change a thing. You got to keep living it out.

Only people with money should care about words

like *truth* or *kindness* or *hate* or *peace*. And in
my experience they're the ones who care the
least. Do you suppose that's how they got their
money?

Doesn't matter. My husband's fool enough for
everyone. You see, I had to protect my invest-
ment. I had to keep Sonny away from him until he was old enough to get what little John
Victor Herbert could offer. Otherwise, he'd
never have wanted it in the first place. John
would have filled him up with false hopes. With
a language that meant absolutely nothing. With
dreams that wouldn't have taken him a single
step. Now that he's old enough, he knows he's
there.

[*She stops her dusting for a moment, pondering
the situation.*]

But where does that leave me? [*Shrugging*] Here,
of course. Where I've always been. Waiting.
Waiting for someplace to go and someone to
take me. Maybe he will, maybe he won't. Only
trouble is, if I get to taste the schnitzel I'll have
lost the appetite. I'll have nothing to say to anyone in the whole of the Italian peninsula. That's
life.

ACT III

The Board Room of Higgins Higgins and Lillian Higgins. Around the table sit the board members, some of whom may be real, others of which are clearly cutouts. At the head of the table stands a very strikingly handsome young man, blonde, almost god-like in his physiognomy.

The action within should be played almost as dance rather than naturalist movement, gesture as opposed to result. Time has been slowed down.

SONNY: Ahhh. Ahhhh. [*He looks down at his notes.*] 1. Ahhhh. [*Again looks down*] 1. Wear a suit. [*He pauses, gradually recognizing the meaning of his words, grinning in that recognition.*] 2. Speak. Ahhh [*looking down*] Welcome.

[*The board members physically relax.*]

SONNY: Welcome. I am Sonny. Ahhhh [*looking down*] I am Sonny. I am happy to be here and to . . . ahhhh . . . [*looking down*] . . . . 1. Wear a suit. [*grinning*] 3. Speak. Reclaim my rightful position as the son of . . . .

[LILLIAN HIGGINS, *enthroned in her wheelchair, bursts into the boardroom,* MR. SMILEY *at her helm. She is a mix of a fairy tale witch and similar characters in the novels of Charles Dickens*].

LILLIAN: You are a fraud!

SONNY: 1. Wear a suit. 2. Speak. I am Sonny, the son of Lillian Higgins and Mr. Higgins.

LILLIAN: You are not my son!

SONNY: 4. Respond. I am your son. I have been away, as many of you know, sent away away ... ahhhh .... 2. Speak.

LILLIAN: You are not my son. My son is dead! [*catching herself*] *believed* dead. The police never found him.

SONNY: I am the son of Lillian Higgins and Mr. Higgins.

LILLIAN: Prove it!

SONNY: Hello. 2. Speak. I am Sonny, the son ....

LILLIAN: I'll hear no more of this. [*Pointing to several of her board members*] Eject him from this room.

FIRST BOARD MEMBER: Now Lillian ....

LILLIAN: Get rid of him! He is not my son!

SECOND BOARD MEMBER: Are you certain, Lillian? He looks a bit like Mr. Higgins. Around the eyes perhaps.

SONNY: 1. Wear a Suit. Ahhhh ....

THIRD BOARD MEMBER: [*a cutout*] Perhaps we should at least hear him out.

LILLIAN: I will have no such shenanigans at my meetings!

FOURTH BOARD MEMBER: You do mean *our* meetings, don't you Lillian, dear.

LILLIAN: I most certainly do not. Remind me to ask for your resignation immediately after the meeting.

FIFTH BOARD MEMBER: [*a cutout*] Do you have any evidence of your birth, son?

SONNY: 2. Speak. I am Sonny . . . ahhh . . . I am happy to be here and to reclaim my rightful position as a son of Lillian Higgins and Mr. Higgins.

LILLIAN: Get rid of him!

[*A momentary silence.*]

SONNY: 5. Speak directly. I am the lawful heir of the company in my father's and mother's names. I am Sonny Higgins, the son of Lillian . . . ahhh . . . [*looking down*] . . . .

LILLIAN: Seize him!

[*A couple of board members attempt to grab hold of him, but he pulls away. Other board members, women and men, grab at him, some in apparent joy at being able to touch him, others in an at-*

138

tempt to hold him. Even SMILEY *can't resist.*]

LILLIAN: [*upbraiding* SMILEY] You fool, take me over there!

[SMILEY *pushes* LILLIAN *and her chair toward* SONNY.]

SONNY: [*attempting to speak, notes in hand*] 1. Wear a suit . . . .

[*As he says this one of the board members grabs him by the coattails, ripping the suitcoat off him. Another grabs at his shirt.*]

SONNY: I am Sonny . . . ahhh . . . the son of Lillian Higgins and Mr. Higgins . . . ahhh . . . . 4. Speak directly.

LILLIAN: This is *not* my son!

[*At that very moment a board member grabs his shirt, which rips away from Sonny's body. The beautiful, suddenly bare-chested creature before them results in a corporate gasp.*]

BOARD MEMBERS: Ahhhhhhh!

MR. SMILEY: He certainly is a handsome young man, Lillian. Are you sure this is *not* your son!

LILLIAN: Idiot! Of course not! [*She lunges toward the boy, revealing a large knife in her right hand.*]

[*Instinctively,* SONNY *puts out his arm to protect himself, accidentally knocking* LILLIAN *from her wheelchair, face down onto the floor.*]

BOARD MEMBERS: Ahhhhhhh! Oh no, someone help us. Someone help us!

[*The board members gather round the fallen and unmoving body of* LILLIAN, *terrified to touch her.*]

BOARD MEMBER 1: What should we do?*

BOARD MEMBER 2: What have you done, son?*

BOARD MEMBER 3: Someone help her up!*

BOARD MEMBER 4: [*a cutout*] Police. Call the Police.*

SONNY: [*blindly attempting to return to order*] 1. Wear a suit. 2. Speak. I am Sonny. I am Sonny.

BOARD MEMBER 5: Be quiet, boy!

[SONNY immediately quiets.]

[SMILEY *gingerly bends to check out his fallen leader.*]

SMILEY: She's dead!

BOARD MEMBER 1: Fallen on her own knife!

BOARD MEMBER 2: Oh my God!

BOARD MEMBER 4: [*a cutout*] Police. Call the Police!

[*All back away, horrified and shocked. Suddenly, all attention is turned upon half-naked giant among them, now totally in tears, absolutely bawling. He bends to the body.*]

SONNY: Mother. Mother! What have I done? What

140

have I done? Mother! [*Turning on the board*] Back off! [*Spreading his body over the fallen Lillian*] Mother! What have I done?

BOARD MEMBER 3: [*attempting to comfort him*] It was not intentional.

BOARD MEMBER 2: No, son. You didn't mean to do this. This was her doing.

BOARD MEMBER 3: She was an evil woman.

BOARD MEMBER 4: [*cutout*] She was a bitch!

SONNY: What have I done?

BOARD MEMBER 1: She came here to stop you.

BOARD MEMBER 3: She called you a fraud!

BOARD MEMBER 4: [*cutout*] She was a bitch. Someone should call the police.

BOARD MEMBER 2: Please don't blame yourself.

SONNY: [*inconsolable*] Mother! What have I done?

BOARD MEMBER 1: I call this meeting back to order [*Gavelling all to quiet except* SONNY.] Order. Order!

    [SONNY *is silenced.*]

BOARD MEMBER 3: Point of order.

BOARD MEMBER 1: Yes.

BOARD MEMBER 3: We had given this meeting over to the rightful heir of this organization, and I think we should not preempt our own previous resolution.

BOARD MEMBER 2: Are we certain, however, that he *is* the rightful heir?

BOARD MEMBER 1: Who else could he be? He called her Mother. No one I have ever known has called her that, not even Smiley here.

SMILEY: I beg your pardon.

BOARD MEMBER 4: [*cutout*] Indeed you should. Has no one noticed anything about this handsome, in fact gloriously beautiful, young man?

SMILEY: He *is* handsome.

BOARD MEMBER 1: He is beautiful.

BOARD MEMBER 3: But is he legally . . . .

BOARD MEMBER 4: [*cutout*] Look upon his back.
[*All board members arise to do so, carefully and puriently examining him.*]

BOARD MEMBER 1: Very, very nice.

BOARD MEMBER 2: Quite muscular. Quite.

BOARD MEMBER 3: A perfect specimen.

BOARD MEMBER 4: He has a small mole upon his upper lumbar shoulder blade. Notice?
[*The Board explores it with their fingers.*]

BOARD MEMBER 4: Didn't Sonny, the son of Lillian Higgins and Mr. Higgins have just such a small mole on his upper lumbar shoulder blade? I remember reading something in the doctor's infant medical report.

BOARD MEMBER 1: Why of course!

BOARD MEMBER 2: If only I'd remembered that!

BOARD MEMBER 5: That proves it absolutely. It proves everything!

BOARD MEMBERS: [*in unison*] Hooray! Hooray!

> [*Several board members help the young* SONNY *up and bring him, half-naked as he is — to stand again before them.*]
>
> [*Silence*]

BOARD MEMBER 5: Speak, son!

SONNY: Ahhhh. My mother . . . [*temporarily breaking down again*] . . . . My mother was not an easy woman to live with. I . . . I needed to get away. But I loved her. I always loved her, and, at times, even missed her [*becoming quickly more and more glib in his speech*]. How many times, how many, I wanted to return, to be here at her side. With you [*spreading out his hands*] all of you dear souls. But, as you all know, she was not easy to live with. She had, how can we not but admit it, a fatal flaw. She was inflicted — there is no other way to express it but through honesty — one might almost say, infected with usuary. She was a . . . ahhhhh . . . money-grabbing, gouging, beast, whose every waking moment was spent on plotting how to get more

143

money, more clothes, more houses, more jewelry, more employees — more power. *In* and *out* of that illness she attempted to murder me by implanting my body, drugged, against his will, by my father, into a large block of wet cement. But before it could completely harden, Mr. John Victor Herbert, a loyal employee of this great institution, chipped away for hours at that block to free me. And here I am today!

BOARD MEMBERS: Hooray!

SONNY: But I love her still. And I can only regret that she has died in such a way. We shall give her Christian burial even if, God forbid she had known this, she would have turned over in her grave.

BOARD MEMBERS: Hooray!

SONNY: But I remember another Lillian, another Mother. At a time before she had become infected with this usurious disease. As a young boy, I was taken on a long sea voyage with my Mother and my Father to Europe, Asia, and the Orient. We crossed the Tigris, the Ganges, the great Kan Yangtze. We ate boars head in Burma and in Bangkok drank a beer they called Pen Sak. She was radiant, peaceful there. Beautiful as the young girl she once was. I loved her more

144

than anything then.

BOARD MEMBERS: Hooray . . . !

BOARD MEMBER 1: [*interrupting the revelry*] New business!

SONNY: May I suggest, no propose. Request. Yes, request that hereafter we deal only in products related to cows.

BOARD MEMBER 4: Pardon?

BOARD MEMBER 2: He said cows.

BOARD MEMBER 3: *Cows?*

BOARD MEMBER 1: May I remind you, sir, we are an ad agency.

SONNY: [*reflecting for a moment, then quite authoritatively*] Then we shall deal only with companies who need ads for cows!

SMILEY: [*unable to control his enthusiasm about the young President*] Hear, hear!

BOARD MEMBER 1: If you believe . . . that is a profitable venture.

SONNY: I do.

BOARD MEMBER 1: Then I'm behind it.

BOARD MEMBER 2: So am I.

BOARD MEMBERS ALL: Hooray!!!! Hoorayyy!!!

In the midst of further cheers and to-do, the curtain falls.

THE SORRY PLAY: A RITUAL

for Cristina Mutarelli and Lígia Cortez

    An arguing couple.

BILL: I'm sorry.

BETTE: For what?

BILL: Sorry. Just sorry.

BETTE: You can't just be sorry.

BILL: Why?

BETTE: It's just the way it works. You have to have something to be sorry about.

BILL: I'm sorry I don't have something to be sorry about.

BETTE: You're silly.

BILL: I'm sorry I'm silly.

BETTE: Stop!

BILL: Sorry. Can't stop.

BETTE: Why do you want to be so sorry?

BILL: I don't know. I just feel I need to be.

BETTE: But you can't just be sorry for such trivial things. You have to have done something —

something wrong, something bad — to be truly sorry.

BILL: [*Thinking for a moment, goes over to* BETTE *and stands beside. Suddenly he pushes his shoulder into her side; she stumbles away, almost falling in the act.*]

BETTE: What are you doing?

BILL: [*with a great look of satisfaction on his face*] I'm sorry I elbowed you like that.

BETTE: Actually, it was your *shoulder*. That hurts! It really hurt!

BILL: I'm sorry I "shouldered" you like that!

BETTE: You're crazy!

BILL: I'm sorry I hurt you.

BETTE: You didn't *really* hurt me. But you're crazy!

BILL: I'm sorry I'm crazy.

BETTE: Please! Please! No more. You can't intentionally do something to be sorry. Or if you do it has to be something, something really to be sorry about. You can't just go around knocking people over just to apologize to them. That's hypocritical. Your being sorry has no significance. [BETTE *turns away in frustration.*]

BILL: [*Pondering for a moment. He walks over to* BETTE *and calmly puts his hands around her neck and begins to choke her to death.*]

BETTE: [*Kicking and flailing about*] Help! Stop! [*She speaks spasmodically, her words garbled.*] Help! Stop! Help!

[*She is nearly done for when suddenly BILL stops. She lurches forward in a grand gasp and, bent over, breathes in heavily for a few seconds.*]

BILL: I'm sorry! I'm sorry. I'm sorry. I don't know what got into me.

BETTE: [*Recovering, she recoils from him*] You're mad! You're *truly* mad!

BILL: I'm sorry. I'm sorry. I really am.

BETTE: No! I won't accept your apologies for that! You've gone too far. You almost did me in!

BILL: [*Suddenly on his knees*] Please! Please! Forgive me. [*Whimpering*] Please! I'm sorry! I didn't mean to do it. Please!

BETTE: There's a limit you know? There's a line. And you've gone over it!

BILL: Please! [*Crying*] Please! I love you. I'm sorry! I'm sorry!

BETTE: I don't know. I mean, you nearly killed me! What would you have done then? Who'd have cooked your black beans and ham-hocks. Who'd have made your bed?

BILL: [*Looking up at her in anguish*]

BETTE: Who'd have washed and ironed your

clothes? Cut your toenails once a month? Scratched your back? Who'd have done that?

BILL: I'm sorry! I'm truly sorry.

BETTE: You have a screw loose.

BILL: I guess.

BETTE: What is this all about? Wanting to be sorry so suddenly?

BILL: I don't know.

BETTE: Well — I, think you *do*!

BILL: What do you mean?

BETTE: Usually when people feel sorry for something they have done something to be sorry about. Like I said.

BILL: I just did something to be sorry for.

BETTE: No! That was just a decoy. A cover-up. You wanted to be sorry because you *were* sorry about something, weren't you?

BILL: I don't understand. You're not making sense.

BETTE: O, I'm not, am I? Tell me. You can tell me. Go ahead.

BILL: What? Tell you what?

BETTE: What you really have to be so sorry about.

BILL: For choking you.

BETTE: Come on, 'fess up.

BILL: I'm sorry for shouldering you out of the way.

BETTE: And before *that*?

149

BILL: [*Confused*] For . . . wanting to be sorry? Yes, I'm sorry for wanting to be sorry.

BETTE: You better be quick about it, or I'll make you sorry.

BILL: I already am. I said I was.

BETTE: That's not enough! I want you to tell me why, why are you so sorry.

BILL: I just did!

BETTE: I mean the *real* reason.

BILL: The *real* reason?

BETTE: Yes. Yes. [*She taps her foot in impatience.*]
[BILL *looks left and right, as if seeking the answer to her demand.*]

BETTE: Yes! That you've been having an *affair!*

BILL: An affair?

BETTE: Yes. Admit it!

BILL: With whom?

BETTE: I don't know. Your secretary maybe.

BILL: I don't have a secretary.

BETTE: Someone else's secretary then!

BILL: I don't know any secretaries — except the boss' — and the boss doesn't allow him to talk to us much.

BETTE: A shopgirl!

BILL: I don't know any shopgirls.

BETTE: Someone's wife. A colleague perhaps? The wife of the boss?

BILL: No. No! I haven't had an affair with any of them.

BETTE: I want the truth!

BILL: It *is* the truth.

BETTE: [*Thinking for a moment, then looking him over head to toe*] I don't think it's possible, but these days you never know. Have you been with another man?

BILL: Another *man*?

BETTE: Answer me!

BILL: Every day — but, no, no — not sexually. Are you asking me if I'm *gay*?

BETTE: I need to know what you have to be so sorry about.

BILL: For years and years every day I come home and kiss you on the cheek. At night we have sex — good sex I thought. Every Friday I hand over to you every cent of my paycheck. And now you wonder if I have been running around with some queen — some *fag* — a motorcycle man?!

BETTE: [*Defiantly*] It happens!

BILL: When would I work?

BETTE: Lunch time — at lunch you could go to a hotel or some secluded spot.

BILL: When would I eat?

BETTE: [*Turning away from him*] Some people go without lunch.

BILL: I need my lunch. Without lunch, my stomach growls. I get light-headed.

BETTE: I know. I know.

BILL: [*Self-righteously*] And where is there a secluded spot in which I could have sex — in this warped picture of me — with some other man?

BETTE: In a park. The woods. I have heard they have sex in toilets, storerooms, empty offices!

BILL: You seem to know an awful lot about their habits.

BETTE: I saw a documentary.

BILL: And you . . . have you gone without lunch — recently I mean?

BETTE: [*Turning back to him in shock*] Nooooooooo!

BILL: After all these years do I deserve so much distrust?

BETTE: [*Pouting*] No.

BILL: Have I been a good husband?

BETTE: Yes. [*A beat*] Yes.

[*A pause*]

BETTE: I'm sorry. [*Long pause*] I'm sorry. I'm really sorry.

BILL: Come here, old girl. [*She comes and he hugs her to him.*] Come. It's time for bed.

A MAN SHOOTING
OR THREATENING TO SHOOT

(suggested by Gertrude Stein's *Mrs. Reynolds*)

[*A chorus of women throughout*]

ACT I
Act of Kindness

A man shooting or threatening to shoot with a gun
  is carrying a calf. There is no major.
Of course . . . if there had been a war . . . .
Not to be afraid at home is always something.
It was yesterday for example, and we were occu-
  pied by being. Girls sit in the dirt and boys eat
  berries. That's always.
And then like a bolt out of the sky it comes to
  us . . .
That is the way it is just then.
Once in a while it has rained for twenty-eight days

not what you had expected.

My o my there are bullets yes or do I mean pel-
lets?

It makes it difficult, difficult to stop whatever it is
you were wanting to.

The man shooting or threatening to shoot.

For example if I were to say get that gun out of
here . . . .

Perhaps she did not often cry but I have seen her
a number of times.

Christmas said Mrs. Carol is unreasonable.

Easter too. The man shooting or threatening to
shoot is carrying a rabbit on his back.

On his way back.

Too late to have come. Too late!

Of course it is neither that or not whatever it
should have been.

Nor is it never.

A loud noise.

Exactly. Exactly.

For example if I were to say . . . .

On some trees evidently there are initials not of
lovers but of men who did not have the opportunity to be.

Some winds bring no harm others only omens.

Has the winter come soon soon?

ACT II
Act of Love

Every day gets to bake a cake. Almost.
She was meditating.
But nobody had to say. Nobody had.
It was as if it were without looking what it really
    had promised to be.
Sing for us Mrs. Carol please
Do.

> He was only forty-eight
> He was only three feet high
> He was just a little fat
> He was maybe more than that
> For when he said goodbye
> He was already late.

Ducks are easy to surprise but absolutely neces-
    sary to.
A man shooting or threatening.
I didn't see her cry but I know she must have had
    to.
They were at the corner just hanging there, just
    hanging out at the corner as if they had noth-
    ing else to do and already had done that.
I was going to bake a cake but put up a pie to

please you instead just to please you.
My o my they were mellets or maybe mallards?
For example . . .
It must have rained for forty-eight days but the
    sun still came out every night.
Of course . . . if there had been a peace.
Of what?
Of what sort?
He has an elephant on his lap!
Goodnight. Goodnight everybody.
Goodnight.
Now it is snowing.

ACT III
Act of Defiance

A very high ridge upon which we can see an ab-
    solutely white horse, held at bay by a man in a
    white coat and black very black gloves hold-
    ing the horse at bay with a rein of very black
    cord or hemp but not a chain that would be too
    brutal no not a chain. But very black. He and
    the horse standing there just standing in a frieze
    and will perhaps if they don't get moving but
    can't being at the back of the stage where would

157

they go if they did rage up the stallion with his front legs in air and the man on the back of the beast just hanging there? Where?

She was meditating.

Then she was very busy again. In love with someone someone said but who no one knew. Everyone was afraid to.

What I say is true. Eggs have to be beaten. That's the way it is. If you don't you won't have what you wanted them to do.

There! On the ridge can you see?

A man shooting or threatening to shoot is not a major.

But he might as well be.

O prayer dear prayer I pray for a brighter day.

Everybody I assure you is going to be astonished, just astonished.

And of course, there is a loud noise. A very loud noise.

Goodnight. You better get inside the way it looks to me.

Ducks are easy to surprise.

While she was out she saw that everybody was out and soon there wasn't anyone anymore so she knew that there wasn't any reason anymore to be where she was.

She was meditating.
He was watching TV.
The children too.
On his back he carries a goose.
Dear Mrs. Carol will you sing?
I have no inclination to.
You might as well since no one else can carry a
tune.
Everyday is milk.
Everyday is cake or pie or cookies.
Ham. Everyday. Cherries. Everyday.
And then you pull out the plum.
That is the way you play.

ACT IV
Act of Congress

She scratched her nose which itched.
She knew something was up.
That is the way it was.
I am anxious she said. I am anxious because I
guess something is up having just scratched my
nose.
He no longer remembered whether she was very
strong or very weak or what day they met or

even if they had yet.

Dear John. I hope everything is what you say it is where you are there.

Dear Mark.

Dear Paul please tell me do you have a coat? I mean a parka perhaps. An alpak. You need one I am sure you do.

Dear Mrs. Carol.

Dear dark December day.

Dear me.

Yes, do go away. Do. I cannot remember why but it is exactly what must be done if something needs to be as evidently you claim it does.

Eggs have to be beaten one by one.

Is the man shooting or threatening to shoot?

Every day is another day.

Why should two men sit in a meadow? Why should two blackbirds sit on his shoulders? Why should two meadows sit on the blackbird's head?

If ducks are easy to surprise do you imagine swans are too? I imagine them, really I do.

They are very comforting.

Very.

If you keep scratching your nose like you're going to have a rash.

A red rose.
I forgot to tell you . . .
Please do.

ACT V
Act of Desperation

War and revolution, revolution and war.
That is a very nasty habit.
Something is up I just know it's something.
The children are all watching TV.
Why I am just speechless. Just!
Over there there is a large patch of ice on which
sits a frozen swan frozen in what must once
have been a patch of water not yet frozen but
soon to be quick for the swan did not evidently
have the time to swim away or fly perhaps if
swans can.
This is a very ominous sign I assure you. It is hard
to bake on a day you know something is up
but isn't evidently yet.
Goodnight. Now the sun can set.
Exactly.
A loud noise! Or perhaps . . .
Shhhhhhhh . . . . Shhhhhhh . . . .

Spring had come and Mrs. Rumor was in the air.
Love to. I would most certainly be glad.
Dear Mark. How are you passing the day today?
That man is threatening.
For example, if you have berries you use them. If
    you have apples too. If you have sugar you are
    a better woman than I could ever be.
The era of peace without iron will surely have
    come to the land if only he comes home as soon
    as he can.
Goodnight.
Now it is raining for forty-eight nights and
    twenty-eight days.
How old do you imagine some soldiers to have
    been?
I do not imagine them.
Then you are a better man.
Goodnight.
Good day.

ACT VI
Act of Belligerence

Weep and wail. Weep and wail.
A man shooting or threatening to shoot with a gun

does what he promises to.

On his way back.

The stage is very dark so dark that you cannot see anything practically nothing until one woman lights a match and puts it to her face and then you can see only her face and nothing else hardly anything but her face since it is the only thing you can see in the dark. Then well anything might happen but here is what I suggest. Another woman puts a match beside her face as well and another and another again until you have several faces lit and then one by one all the matches go out until you are in the dark again.

This was the first speech I had ever made. It said My dearest ones can you believe we have been here all along without even knowing it and now it is hard to believe we have ever left, knowing, sometimes secretly that we are still here where we shouldn't be but having nowhere else to go haven't yet left.

That was very comforting dear.

Wail and weep. Wail and weep.

Do sing for us Mrs. Carol. Mrs. Rumor tell us a tale.

Well, once there was a rabbit who was very happy

and agile and fast and ran around as quick as he could through everybody's cabbage patch and they didn't really mind because there was a lot of cabbage to be had until they no longer had eggs or sugar and since they didn't they didn't have cakes or pies anymore either or cookies. Certainly not hams. Cherries and other berries were very dear. So cabbage came to be. And suddenly now everyone hated that rabbit who had been so happy and agile and so very fast that someone, a man shooting or threatening to shoot with a gun perhaps carried the rabbit across his back.

Easter too.

Some winds bring no harm.

But others do.

ACT VII
Act of Omission

It looked as if he was going to be late. And then he was.

And when it does. Dear me when it does.

Every day is another day.

Good morning.

Good afternoon.
Weep and wail. Wail and weep.

ACT VII
Act of War

I should have known.
We all should have.
A loud noise. Louder than we thought.
Once in a while I do not even like the stars.
Often. That is the way it is just then.
For example, if I were to say get out of here just
    get out!
Would he have come anyway another day?
He liked Queens.
That was the way it was.
He didn't like Manhattans.
The second family were all friends of the first fam-
    ily and the first family were all friends of the
    third. But the third didn't have anyone else to
    be friends to having lost themselves in the war
    like that.
Exactly. Exactly.
Is it any wonder that the children have no minds
    having watched everything they've seen

through the lens of a hot white tube that says
this is what it is and never bothers even to ask
if it should be and could even be something
else. Is it any wonder that the children are all
deaf?

The noise. The loud noise all night.

Sing Mrs. Carol.

I do not feel like it.

Mark used to recite poetry. I think I remember him
repeating a sonnet in a church. Or maybe it was
my mother's brother.

Once upon a time *I* saw a rainbow.

Once I saw a flower.
Then I saw a plower
plow up that flower
and build a tower
which within an hour
utterly collapsed.

ACT IX
Act of Contrition

Now it was time to go to bed.
Now it was time to soon be dead.
O dear said Mrs. Rumor. O dear!

There might be a sigh when everybody heard that
   someone was marching marching off or marching in where many would never march again.
   Marching marching. Many a man and many a
   woman couldn't.

Silence followed.

On the ridge is a man shooting or threatening to
   shoot without a gun just with his arm and his
   hand. But everyone recognizes him nonetheless.

I am delivering another speech: Dearest nation we
   have all suffered a lot a great deal and much
   more and therefore we have suffered more than
   we deserved to have wherefore I proclaim that
   we shall not suffer anymore never ever not an
   inch.

The men are all watching television.

The women have begun to bake. Some boys. Now
   men. And then whole families. But there is no
   taste.

It is so hot in here today.

It is very hot and unpleasant surely someone can
   say that without being misunderstood.

You have to be careful.

I'd stay inside if I could. But I no longer have one.

Nor I.

A loud noise!

Another?

Yes. Again.

Perhaps it is the one who is marching here or going away. Perhaps it is his brother.

On some trees evidently there are initials not of lovers but of women who did not have the opportunity to be.

That is the way it is just then.

ACT X
Act of God

Shhhhh. Shhhhh.

And when they have dinner today they will have dinner the way they always have dinner. And then they will watch the television again. And then they will go to bed. And then they will be dead. In the morning they will be dead.

That is the way it always has been.

A man shooting or threatening to shoot with a gun . . . carrying another man on his back.

It makes it difficult, difficult to stop whatever it is you are wanting to.

The man shooting or threatening to shoot.

A loud noise.
Exactly.
Shhhhhh. Shhhhhh.

> There was a man whose daughters drowned
> in the waters around the house he lived in
> which clearly he built, O Noah, O Jonah, in a
>   swamp of sin.
> In a swamp of sin. O Peter even you can't deny:
> He built his house to destroy his kin.

Shhhhhh. Shhhhhhhh.

GREEN INTEGER
Pataphysics and Pedantry

Douglas Messerli, *Publisher*

Essays, Manifestos, Statements, Speeches, Maxims,
Epistles, Diaristic Notes, Narratives, Natural Histories,
Poems, Plays, Performances, Ramblings, Revelations
and all such ephemera as may appear necessary
to bring society into a slight tremolo of confusion
and fright at least.

*

GREEN INTEGER BOOKS

1   Gertrude Stein *History or Messages from History* $5.95
2   Robert Bresson *Notes on the Cinematographer* $8.95
3   Oscar Wilde *The Critic As Artist* $9.95
4   Henri Michaux *Tent Posts* $10.95
5   Edgar Allan Poe *Eureka, A Prose Poem* $10.95
6   Jean Renoir *An Interview* $9.95
7   Marcel Cohen *Mirrors* $12.95
8   Christopher Spranger *The Effort to Fall* $8.95
9   Arno Schmidt *Radio Dialogs I* $12.95
10 Hans Christian Andersen *Travels* $12.95
11 Christopher Middleton *In the Mirror of the Eighth
    King* $9.95

Green Integer EL-E-PHANT Books (6 x 9 format)